Southasia Revisited

Essays on Politics, state-building, ethnography, rights and development

Zulfiqar Shah

Createspace, An Amazon Company

ACKNOWLEDGMENTS

This is a compilation of the analytical articles, essays and research papers on various issues of Southasia published in daily The Kathmandu Post, Nepal; daily Republica; Nepal, daily Afghanistan Times, Kabul; and Truthout, USA. The write-are a Sindhian view of Southasia.

CONTENTS

DEDICATED TO SOUTHASIANS

1
FEDERALISM IN PAKISTAN

Federalism in *Southasia* has many forms. Pakistan, Sri Lanka and Afghanistan have remained highly volatile federations in post-colonial *Southasia*; whereas, India, the largest democracy as well as one of the largest federations on the globe, has its own dynamics. Federal practices are being revisited everywhere in the region–reconstruction in Afghanistan, revisions in Pakistan, restructuring in Sri Lanka, constitutional process in Nepal, rethinking over Chittagong in Bangladesh and over Kurdistan and Sistan in Iran.

Pakistan is the only *Southasian* country which been broken in the post-colonial period and is once again under the same threat; therefore it is important to learn from its federal practices, particularly in relation to Sindh, now a province but which was a sovereign country for over 2,000 years until the British set foot in 1843. It not only voluntarily chose to become a part of Pakistan in 1947 but also gave birth to Mohammad Ali Jinnah, the country's Pakistan.

Pakistan is a peculiar federalism with two permanent, conflicting features, which act as foundations of its federal crises. The country runs eight administrative units but looks to secure the interests of only one ethnicity at the cost of others.

The provinces of Sindh and Punjab are almost modern democracies. Balochistan is a tribal administration. Khyber Pakhtunkhuwa (formerly NWFP) has four administrative systems where major cities are modern democracies and the rest is divided into Federally Administered Tribal Areas (FATA), Federal Criminal Regulation Area (FCR or semi tribal areas) and Shariah Law for Mehemend Agency.

This permanent diversity is in keeping with the aspirations of people from different backgrounds; however it was not appropriately reviewed until last year, when FATA was constitutionally given the rights of electoral franchise and political association.

The other permanent feature of federalism in the country is political and legislative arrangements securing dominating majority and economic prosperity of Punjab province over the rest, in what people from other provinces term demographic hegemony. The history of state-building and legislation in Pakistan, basically, revolves around this single factor.

During the partition of India, the majority of All India Muslim League (AIML) supporters from Muslim minority provinces in northern and central India migrated to Pakistan. They were heartily welcomed by Sindhi people. Muhajirs (refugees), as they called themselves, were settled in selective urban hubs of Sindh including Karachi, Hyderabad and Sukkur so as to create constituencies for the immigrant AIML leaders. Therefore ALML leadership favored non-democratic politics.

In 1958, General Ayub Khan took over with the help of civil bureaucracy and AIML leadership and gave the country its first comprehensive constitution. This was followed by the imposition of 'One Unit System' on the basis of parity between eastern and western wings of Pakistan. The East Pakistan Bengalis were a majority in the newly formed Pakistan; therefore, they were countered through the merger of Punjab, Sindh, Balochistan and NWFP into single province of West Pakistan against the will of three latter provinces.

Publishing, reading and writing in Sindhi language was banned during One Unit because Sindhi was the only language in Pakistan which had a script and was the language of academia. Urdu was imposed as a national language, which was resisted by Sindhis and Bengalis. Finally, One Unit had to be abolished due to fear of liberation movement in Bangladesh.

Pakistan was given its third constitution in 1973 by PM Minister Zulfiqar Ali Bhutto who hailed from Sindh. This time, the principle of majority democracy was adopted which suited demographic majority of Punjab. Later on, Bhutto was executed under general Zia's martial law imposed in 1977, which led Sindh into a decade-long resistance that was countered through a five-pronged strategy of militarization; criminalization through dacoits; creating tribal fiefdoms in non-tribal Sindh districts; encouraging ethnic violence by Muhajirs in Karachi and Hyderabad; and managing demographic influx of Afghan refugees and Punjabis to Sindh. At one stage during this process, the military was transformed into a separate interest group, and the political process of 1990's in Pakistan was basically marked by conflict between civilian and non-civilian actors.

The post 9/11 Pakistani federalism attempts a viable statehood. But the genesis of separatism are still there, as was evident in the Dec 27, 2007 assassination of Benazir Bhutto, when Pakistan ceased to exist in Sindh for three days and nights; however, mass uprising were soon overpowered by Asif Zardari, husband and political successor of Benazir Bhutto. Sindh and Balochistan today are strongholds of freedom movements. Murders of

Sindhi nationalist leaders and enforced disappearances of hundreds of political and rights activists has become a routine.

Sindh's experience with federalism offers some important lessons. Only a federalism that offers political pluralism and ethnic as well as demographic securities can have permanence. Federation entails just distribution of resources, right to rule, maintaining demographic majority and appropriate share in all forms of statecraft and power in historic land. If a federation develops a foreign policy without accommodating people's and especially federating states' will, the consequences can be disastrous. *Southasia*n countries' varied experiences in federalism can be shared to each country's benefit, including Nepal.

Identities are also important in single-nation countries, although of an entirely different nature. In Nepal and Bangladesh districts or divisions are administrative provinces, therefore their development and economic viability is a matter of high importance. In case of disagreement, mediation, consultation and understanding between conflicting administrative units are the solution. One of the long-running disputes in Sindh over the division of Larkana district was resolved when the newly formed district of Shahdadkot was jointly named 'Qambar-Shahdadkot' after mediation.

*Southasia*n countries have versatile experiences of federal practices and we can share them for each other's benefits. Why not facilitate this through establishment of a *Southasia*n Court of Justice and *Southasia*n Forum of Federating States under SAARC or any other arrangement? Such a body can help devise conflict resolution mechanisms and by doing so eliminate the chances of violence, dismemberments and political conflicts in federations of *Southasia*.

There are many conflicts within federations in Africa, resolution of which would be a milestone towards, peace, development and human security. In fact, the United Nations could be a legitimate forum for this, but it gives legitimate mandate only to sovereign countries, whereas the unresolved issues among federating states or between centre and federating state are almost non-addressable in the forum. Thus restructuring of the United Nations in which federating states may be given legitimate space for reconciliation and resolution of disputes is urgently needed.

Published in Daily Republica, Nepal on July 22, 2012

2
SAVING SOUTHASIA: IMPACTS OF CLIMATE CHANGE

Climate change is likely to wreak havoc in *Southasia* and along two climate vulnerable points—Himalaya in the north and a vast coastline in the South. The foundation of the 'oneness' in this ecologically diverse and volatile region lies in it being an integrated climate entity with the same regional plateau, shared ecology and interdependent natural resources—mainly rivers. Besides, from the civilization point of view, the boundaries of the region are historically bracketed between Gango-Jaumna and Sindhu-Sarsvati civilizations.

Glacial northern in Himalaya, which is the mother of all rivers in the region, forms 67 percent of global glacial mass. The densely populated river plains and coastlines might just be the worst examples of human disaster because of global warming and steady snowmelt, which is the primary cause of floods and could ultimately result in acute water scarcity.

Besides, rising sea levels in coastlines is bound to destroy the deltaic areas and frequent storms, cyclones and unexpected heavy downpours in the southern areas, along with sparse rainfall and dryness in the north central, has already begun.

This scenario is bound to cause major changes in crop patterns altering the agricultural foundations of the region, heavy displacements due to floods, increasing migrations due to livelihood loss and disharmonized ecological and biodiversity compositeness in the region, which will ultimately give birth to inter- as well as intra-state conflicts. These conflicts, in turn, will cause livelihood and food insecurities and diversification of ethnic fabric of various federations and federating states. This will also lead to mounting pressure on major cities across the region and finally, make the region prone to various forms of natural disasters along with predictable social catastrophes.

The current floods in India in which millions are affected is only a small version of what happened during 2010-11 in Pakistan in which almost 20 million people were displaced in Sindh province alone within two years, causing the biggest ever humanitarian crisis of the region. Bangladesh, which usually faces massive floods, will now touch the fringes of severities. Sri Lanka is and will be threatened by the rising sea level and it is believed the Maldives may just vanish from the world map. Conflicts over Kabul River may increase between Afghanistan and Pakistan, and conflicts over shared waters between India-Pakistan, India-Nepal and India-Bangladesh may further intensify.

In Pakistan, Sindh has already become a microcosmic picture of this *Southasian* climate big bang, witnessing the fourth highest recorded temperature on the globe in 2010 at 52.8 °C, increasing precipitation in its north and South-eastern areas along with lowering precipitation in the South-western hilly arid belt including Karachi city, decline in the subsoil water table, infrequent rainfalls and erratic Indus floods combined with squeezed springs and autumns. This has given birth to a severe social and humanitarian disaster with 200 million people displaced and damages that are still being evaluated in hundreds of billion dollars.

The Indus Delta has already been destroyed during the last three decades where nearly two million acre fertile land has been intruded by sea water, causing a loss of US $180 million dollars to the province along with mass migration of nearly half a million people. Socio-economic upheavals caused by the situation are putting increasing pressure on the cities, aggravating possibilities of conflicts and it is expected that a huge migration to Sindh due to severe dryness in Punjab in the next decade will further intensify the conflict between Sindh and Punjab and possibly give birth to water wars between the provinces.

Security, if seen in non-military strategic terms, includes the statecraft of ensuring a food and livelihood regime, economic prosperity and peace for sustainable human and social development, guarantying greater people's sovereignty. Climate change is going to challenge our human development compactness, create humanitarian crises and lead to infrastructure devastation along with demographic and economic destabilization. It can result in governance failure and lead to civil wars and socio-political fragmentations.

Responding to the challenge, a wider regional framework is required that should ideally begin with the joint Climate Research Centre at Himalayan Nepal along with the establishment of a highly rich Scientific Council of concerned scientists, experts, researchers and recognized academicians.

The salts of nation states are put to test during this crisis, where no individual country of the region can devise a countrywide framework, which minimizes the threats and addresses the impacts simultaneously. Therefore, a regional framework and regional course of action and intervention is required.

Besides, the mode of production in the region—in general and of agriculture, livestock, fisheries and forestry in particular—needs to be reassessed in the given situation because a majority of population in the region is rural, which has a larger share in our economies. A major crop pattern shift accompanied by market aspect may cause vulnerabilities. This cannot be done in isolation and requires a regionally as well as locally judicious and sustainable distribution, use and utilization of shared water resources.

Along with the high temperature seeds and fish breeds, irrigation methods and technologies ensuring economic use of water could be adopted at higher levels. Such initiatives are already being adopted, although in a limited way, in India, Bangladesh and Pakistan. A climate change framework of health and hygiene requires more focus as people across the region are becoming more prone to climate change-related health issues and diseases.

What is also needed is a *Southasia* Treaty on shared water resources, followed by the countrywide Water Acts regulating judicious distribution of water resources among the federating states and between upper and lower riparian regions.

Climate change will challenge the human development, create a humanitarian crises and lead to various kinds of destabilization.

The majority of the population in the region resides near the coastlines and therefore, a Regional Coastline Agreement is needed for off-shore natural resource explorations, tsunami and cyclone pre-emptive plans and information sharing, digitalizing fishing boats with transmitters and early warning systems, banning reclamation of land in the sea and finally, to address rising sea levels.

Centres of excellence in climate change studies should be established in the vulnerable states or the regions. Besides, India, Pakistan and Bangladesh should come forward to engage with upper space notations for regional level research.

Saving *Southasia* would ultimately mean saving the globe. But this will be impossible until we revisit SAARC and convert it into a regionally active body.

Published in Daily Republica, Kathmandu, Nepal. July 22, 2012

3

SOUTHASIAN RENAISSANCE: LAND ISSUES IN SOUTHASIA

Unlike in the rest of the world, land is the common and most important factor behind modern state building, political culture, socioeconomic development and transformation, urbanization and ethnic conflicts in *Southasia*n countries.

Shared climate, water and natural resources along with broader ethnic similarities are not the only bonds among the people of this region; it is primarily land, and thereby economy and culture, that shapes the universality of *Southasia*. The division is only in the governance and security, which necessitates borders.

The landmass in the region is the sign of its richness, with 4.77 million square kilometres of land offering 2.62 million square kilometres for agriculture. Out of the total land in *Southasia*, 39 percent land is arable, 11 percent comprises permanent pastures and 17 percent is forest and wood land, according to World Bank and FAO studies.

Political dynamics of land are embodied in the political economy; however with two major factors across the region—the unjust land utilization and management, pushing 500 million rural people into the web of vulnerability; and 60 percent human mass depending on land related livelihood. Nepal and Bhutan's 90 percent, Bangladesh's 71.9 percent, India and Pakistan's 70 percent and Sri Lanka's 37 percent population is rural and their livelihood, directly or indirectly, is associated with land. Agriculture contributes 25 percent to the GDP of the region.

Keeping 28 percent urban mass of the region in the background, which will double up over the next decade, it can be seen that the region and its countries are undergoing a massive transformation in human history that was only witnessed before during the renaissance era in Europe. The socio-economic transformation always carries with it a degree of political turmoil, breakthroughs in fields of science, arts and literature and always culminates into new social contracts, though after many conflicts.

Will the region and countrywide gradual transformations be in unison across the board? Will there be new social contracts in individual countries or will a collective will and identity of the region emerge as well? And finally, will this transformation be able to address crucial questions including inter-state conflicts, national questions within the federations, class dynamics, manmade religious antagonism and finally, the collective niche for a universal view of *Southasia*?

Land in *Southasia* has many contours. The rural population in almost all countries of the region is chained under feudal and semi-feudal relations that are shared by the feudal lords with the capitalist and emerging urban population. The latter, juxtaposing its historical essence, has been minimizing the velocity of transformation; mostly due to the nexus between land and power which strengthened during the state building process in various countries of the region.

Land and land related population today is facing pressing issues that include land concentration, increase in landlessness, rural unemployment and consequently migration, residential land insecurities and increasing commercialization of land, occupation of public land by security forces and government departments, bonded labour, agriculture pricing and wages as well as degradation of land.

The extensive urbanization process in the region is mostly cantered in India, Pakistan and Bangladesh and is gripped by land related chaos; therefore, urban land management along with national land policies in the region is unavoidable.

Besides, land has become a major source of conflict—in Nepal and India it is between various ethnic, social and tribal groups; in Bangladesh, it exists because of land scarcity and in Pakistan, due to various forms of land grab by the ethnic militants and mafia in the urban areas, feudal lords in the rural hubs and security forces in the whole country.

Peasantry, rural population and civil society of the region have been struggling to tackle issues related to land rights. The ongoing yearlong Jan Satyagarha by Ekta Parishad in India, the two week-long 'Sindh Peasants Long March' for tenancy legislation in Sindh in 2009, fishing communities movement in coastal districts of Sindh in 2005, resistance by the peasants of Okara military form in Punjab in the last decade in Pakistan, and the Kirshok movement in Bangladesh are documented examples of the struggle around land and rural livelihood rights.

Apart from being the core of power, politics and state formation in *Southasia*, land is also a major source of livelihood, food security and housing. The region shares the colonial land utilization legacy rooted in the highly land concentrated feudalism. Post-colonial *Southasia*n states built and transformed themselves through majority of landholding aristocracy. Therefore, until the land rights regime is not appropriately addressed, achieving inclusive and pluralistic democracies, enduring peace as well as sustainable food sovereignty and security in the region will be impossible.

Land and agrarian reforms in the region should be carried out by focusing on 'land security', including the sustainable use and utilization of land, a 'rights' framework and prevailing food sovereignty.

The nexus of power and land needs to be redefined by transforming land from being a source of socio-political influence into the source of collective prosperity, ensuring economic well being of the majority and their participation in the democratic process. Besides, decentralization of land combined with land entitlement rights and redistribution of land to the landless poor can help the region in resolving local conflicts and increasing agricultural productivity.

Urban land utilization and land commercialization should carefully be regularized to ensure the rights of indigenous communities and adequate housing, as well as establishing ecologically vibrant human settlements.

Agricultural labour and peasantry should legislatively be recognized as labour and provided with social security along with the right to form trade unions for collective bargaining. By altering existing legal frameworks of the tenure and tenancy concerning peasantry, appropriate legislation should be introduced according to existing realities and needs. Besides, a judicial mechanism for peasants and agriculture workers should be established, similar to the labour courts.

The land rights of tribal, forest and indigenous communities particularly of Dalits, women and minorities should be ensured. Bonded labour and other forms of slavery in *Southasia* should be abolished.

Agriculture should be modernized sustainably to enhance production but land grabbing in the name of corporate agriculture farming should not be permitted. Agriculture land utilization must be linked with the sustainable and judicious use of water resources. Given the climate volatility of the region, land acquisition in sea waters should be banned and marine natural resources exploration should be stopped.

Time has come for a *Southasia*n movement around land rights; and the civil society of the region needs to respond to it. It is the prime responsibility of *Southasia*n Association for Regional Cooperation (SAARC) to adopt a charter for land rights, which should be agreed upon and followed by the all stakeholders to ensure land security in the region.

Renaissance of *Southasia* is not a dream. It is deeply rooted in the socio-economic and political development of the region, which is underway—although slow paced, and state and governance reforms as well as new social contracts. Here, SAARC has to play a major role in fostering the discussion about the dynamics of social transformation, economic development and interdependency within the region.

Published in Daily Republica, Kathmandu, Nepal on July 10, 2012

4
BEYOND REGIONALISM: EVOLVING SOUTHASIA

Beyond the much touted culture mantra, it is the political legacy combined by the geo-economic factors and emerging strategic shifts in the global trends that determines the future of contemporary *Southasia*. Political legacy in terms of state building, statehood and statecraft along with social process of development vis-à-vis state organism is the key towards understanding this highly dynamic region. No doubt, despite huge inter- as well as intra-state disparities from the development point of view, the region offers great prospects for social and economic leadership in the world.

The region shares similar development patterns, however, with certain peculiarities of each country's political economy. *Southasia* houses 22 percent of the global population, makes for 2 percent of Global GDP and 1.3 percent of world trade—and accounts for 44 percent of the poverty-stricken segment of the globe, as compared to Sub-Saharan Africa which is home to 46 percent of the world's poor.

Pakistan offers an example of a country which offers various juxtapositions in the course of its development. It is systematically underperforming on most social and political indicators including education, health, sanitation, fertility, gender equality, corruption, political instability and violence, and democracy vis-à-vis its GDP per capita growth over time, aptly named 'growth without development.' These inequalities are basically between various provinces and their ethnicities; urban and rural regions; and socio-politically marginalized and powerful groups. This is one of the main contributors to intra-state conflict, violence and politically instability in Pakistan; similar situation prevails in other countries of the region.

If only one indicator of labour force is taken into consideration, the dire situation becomes evident. According to the Labour Force Survey 1982-83, 28 percent of the employed labour force had attained formal education in Pakistan, while the current population of the formally educated makes up 43 percent. But the pattern of growth in educated labour force is not uniform in all four provinces. Sindh had the highest level of literacy a couple of decades ago; Balochistan had the lowest literacy level for the employed labour force. The gap between the literacy level of Sindh and the provinces of Punjab and Khyber Pakhtunkhwa, has been further skewed in recent times. This is because Sindh's educated mass has grown at a decreasing rate due to political instability in the province as well as the centre's inability to support the region.

Similar is the case, however, on relatively lower scale and with slightly different nature, with other countries of the region particularly India, Bangladesh, Sri Lanka and Nepal, where underdeveloped Northeast in India, Southeast in Bangladesh, Northwest in Sri Lanka and mountainous population of Nepal face socioeconomic marginalization and underdevelopment. This has resulted in a range of intra-state conflicts in the region that includes Kashmir, Jharkhand and Assam vs. Delhi in India; mountainous tribes of Chittagong vs. Dhaka in Bangladesh; Mountainous vs. Tarai people in Nepal; Tamil vs. Sinhala majority in Sri Lanka; and Balochistan and Sindh vs. Islamabad in Pakistan.

Achieving stability and prosperity in the region calls for a multi-pronged approach. The unavoidable change in the anatomy and chemistry of state organism as well as the nature of federalism so as to level the playing field of polity and development may be provided through judicious distribution of resources to the marginalized classes, ethnicities and social groups. Besides, it essentially requires inter-state arrangements that positively enhance the productive interdependency and interwoven social fabric; and finally a regional socioeconomic policy and collectively agreed tangible plan along with its political and structural armaments that ensures the sustenance of the region as a progressive economic and leading cultural region in the world.

The countries in the region desperately require major reforms that help detach its colonial strings and transform it from an oligarchy to the people's state offering maximum federalism. This is the only way to foster equitable development in the intrastate context by minimizing intra-state conflicts and domestic instability in the region.

Besides, a wider range of initiatives is required to promote inter-state progressive dependencies which may include the Establishment of a Ministry for *Southasia*n Affairs, Establishing of *Southasia* University with campus in every regional country and a *Southasia*n Media House; *Southasia*n Multiple Visa for the Married Couples belonging to two different countries, construction of *Southasian* Highway from Dhaka to Kabul, Kandahar and Tehran. Similarly, other important initiatives could be establishment of Bank of *Southasia* and initiating *Southasian* Prize Bonds; founding a *Southasian* Sports Board; passports bearing major *Southasian* languages of the region, establishing a *Southasian* Tourism Board; *Southasian* Courts of Justice similar to International Court of Justice; a loose forum like Congress of *Southasian* States/Provincial Government Representatives; and announcement of limited Dual and Multiple nationalities in *Southasia* for senior citizens, journalists, peace activists and divided families.

Additionally, establishment of a *Southasian* Disaster Fund and *Southasian* Scouts to promote volunteerism during natural disasters; establishment of Press Club of *Southasia*; organizing a Collective Forum of the *Southasian* Political Parties; inclusion of *Southasian* languages departments in all public universities and inclusion of *Southasian* Culture and History Department in every major university.

The dream of a promising *Southasia* can only be realized if these initiatives are taken for homogeneous development, interdependency and vibrant social and economic progress across the region. Collective peace and cultural prosperity can yet be attainted through meaningful interdependency.

Published in Daily Republica, Kathmandu, Nepal on June 12, 2012

5
THE NEW NEUTRAL

When individual or collective conflicts push politics into a blind alley, neutrality becomes key to mediation and resolution. Mediation, in all its forms—cultural, individual, collective or judicial—requires neutrality. If seen through the lens of diplomatic history among nations and the cultural history of people, neutrality embodied with justice has not only been successful in bringing about peace but also sustaining it. Hence, the diversified nature of conflicts, inter- as well as intra-state, ethnic and group require the exhibition of extreme neutrality for a judicious and sustainable resolution of the antagonism that is destined to lead all of us towards collective destruction.

No sides to take

Inter- and intra-state, ethnic and national conflicts have frequently occurred in the post-modern world. The post-World War League of Nations, which culminated into the UN, was an outcome of many international/European treaties among nations, which were neither judicious nor brokered by neutral mediators. Hence, it provided a reason for World War II. The two World Wars were waged between colonisers and aspirants holding colonial ambitions, seeking maximum control over colonies and their wealth and natural resources. Thus, the birth of the UN became inevitable since a neutral body was the niche of the modern era of statehood. Meanwhile, the powerful among the countries also formed parallel alliances at regional and international levels to further their interests.

No doubt, the UN has gradually transcended into a comparatively neutral forum since the world needed to go a step forward to formulate an international legal framework, not only for the member states but also for the citizens of member states. However, it is the our duty to introduce further reforms, agree upon new legal and policy frameworks, reform the structure and the authority to exhibit maximum neutrality and impartiality. Nations, governments and international institutions always have to deal with a complex patchwork of relations and behaviours when they have to switch between neutrality and securing their interests. Since national interest has mostly superseded justice and neutrality in interest-based competitions, diplomacy and internal-external engagements, neutrality today has become an absurdity. This was evident in the recent political crises in Syria and Ukraine. It has also been observed in the Israel-Palestine conflict, the Kurdistan Movement, the Tibetan issue and the freedom movement in Sindh and Balochistan in Pakistan. In fact, the absence of justice-based neutrality, both in nation-states and international and regional forums like the UN, Saarc and the Organisation of Islamic Countries, despite coming up with remedies have also been deepening the old wounds of the people. This has resulted in the rise of gross human rights violations, ethnic cleansing and war crimes that victimise millions of innocent citizens and dissenters.

Power biases

Power and interest-based politics and diplomacy have also given birth to another kind of discrimination. It is based on a discriminatory approach towards social leadership from the perspective of the oppressed or less powerful nations and ethnicities vis-à-vis monopolists and the powerful. The phenomenon is exclusively seen in broader civil society, which includes activists, journalists, writers, analysts, intellectuals, lawyers and other professionals. Usually, social leadership, associated with powerful ethnic groups, command more centrality and acceptability than leaders from among the group of oppressed people.

The phenomenon is more visible in the developing world, particularly in *Southasian* societies where social, institutional and structural development has historically been built around power. Pakistan, Bangladesh and Nepal are the best examples of this tilt. Since the Pakistani state and power corridors, for example, are monopolised by ethnic Punjabi allied with the Urdu-speaking elite, the rest of the *Southasian* and the world societies have an unintentional bias towards the social leadership of Sindhi, Balochi, Pashtun and Siraki origin vis-à-vis those of Punjabi and Urdu origin. This further intensifies issues of high importance and complex nature. The leadership of Punjabi and Urdu origin in Pakistan is well connected with the state, to which they have historically been given agency to participate in decision making. Their input is usually sought after by the establishment in almost all significant internal and external decision making. Besides, they also defend, in numerous cases, even unjustifiable decisions by the state in international forums in an overt or covert manner.

On the other hand, the leadership from Sindh, Balochistan, Khyber Pakhtunkhuwa and Siraiki Southern Punjab has been contributing intellectually to the social and political movements for rights. The journalists, human rights activists, scholars, intellectuals, academicians and literati from these provinces are not only discriminated within Pakistan but also during professional and thematic forums held regionally and internationally. Similarly, when Baloch or Sindhi journalists, activists and thinkers are persecuted or killed by the state forces, the regional and international media and civil society seldom give them attention. However, when people of Punjabi and Urdu origin from the same professions— which are usually attached to certain layers of the establishment—are victimised, it becomes a matter of concern in regional and international forums. If the Sindhi or Baloch leadership sympathises with the political movement of their people and victims of persecution, the world outside criminalises them. None would even think for the moment that the civil society and media associates and advisors of dominant ethnic groups in Pakistan have also an intellectual share in the crimes against humanity committed by the state. They are generally treated as credible entities. This inability to differentiate between social and civil leadership of the oppressed and the oppressor even by the leadership of other countries is also a kind of bias. Their unwillingness to see perceive both the parties as equals is also a kind of discrimination. It is an exhibition of the people-to-people or civil non-neutrality. This attitude is not only found among individuals but also those in highly reputable rights bodies, media houses, think tanks and intellectuals.

A similar problem persists on a lower scale and in different forms when the leadership from the smaller countries, mostly with a single majority ethnic-construct like Nepal, Bangladesh, the Maldives and Bhutan engage and interact with their counterparts from the rest of the developing world. The non-existence of a neutral human interaction and people-to-people contact are more dangerous than that the foreign policies of the establishments of developing countries. The critical mass of human rights, civil, political and economic justice and peace has grown in the last two decades. This larger tribe of activists, experts, journalists, writers, intellectuals, academicians and other professionals usually identifies itself with the various aspects and levels of social justice. Paradoxically, it lacks justice within its own tribe when it comes to supporting and sympathising with victims or being neutral when it's a case of the oppressed versus the dominant. This not only applies to broader civil society but also international bodies. New ethoses need to replace old biases, discrimination and non-neutrality, primarily in people's diplomacy.

Published in Daily The Kathmandu Post, Nepal on August 10, 2014

6

WHY BRITAIN IS RESPONSIBLE TO THE PEOPLE OF SINDH AND BALOCHISTAN

Scottish people decide their political future according to their will. No doubt it is political civilization of UK due to which it agreed with the Parliament of Scotland for holding a referendum of the union versus secession. It is an important moment when UK also needs to consider its obligations for the political morality concerning its previous colonies.

The previous British colonies are globally in the media lime light today. Conflicts, violence and wars have become commonplace in the regions that were colonized by Great Britain between the seventeenth and nineteenth centuries.

Why after winning freedom in the wake of Second World War, the previous British colonies in Asia are still yearning for the real freedoms, development, peace and human security? The answer can only be found in the design and modus operandi of the colonial rule as well as the Britain's departure strategy from the colonies after 1945. One cannot underestimate, however, the positive contribution of the Britain imperialism of putting the modern foundations of state-building, development and social-transformation in the colonies, which earlier were unable to transform from feudal societies and barter economies into the Industrial and modern one.

Southasia is a highly intelligible and comprehensive example of the prolonged instability among the previous British colonies despite the fact that Iraq and Kuwait in the Middle East have been centre-stage of world politics of conflicts during the last three decades. The partition of Kuwait from the historical Iraqi territory had arguably lesser impacts on the Asian politics of the international interests than that of the partition of the Indian Subcontinent due to South-and-Central Asian strategic contours. This is important to note that like Pakistan there has been no country named 'Iraq' in the history, neither the contemporary Iraqi geography has ever been a sovereign country.

Sri Lanka, Myanmar, Pakistan and Bangladesh have undergone several waves of conflicts, violence, civil rights violations and crimes against humanity, militarization and the wars in the post-colonial era. Mainland India alone has socio-politically elevated to certain extent from such broader instability.

Among *Southasia*n countries, Pakistan is a peculiar case study of the inappropriate, unrealistic and unjustified designs of the Imperial Britain, which have resulted into the broader insecurity for the tens of millions Sindhi, Baloch and Pashtun. The colonial and contemporary unrealistic experiences of the world community with the internal politics of Pakistani ethno-national dynamics have damaged both Sindhi-Baloch-Pashtun and the international community.

Rationality behind Pakistan and the realities

No historian, academician or analyst has hitherto found an appropriate rationale for creating Pakistan. The historical documents note that Pakistan was created on the line of so-called two-nation theory based on Indian Hindu and Muslim nationhood. The idea of Pakistan was rejected by the federating provinces of Sindh, Balochistan, and NWFP (now Khyber Pakhtunkhuwa - KPK), and Siraiki speaking people of Southern Punjab that together form roughly ninety percent of geography and seventy percent of the population of Pakistan.

The founding political party of Pakistan, the All India Muslim League (AIML), never won elections in British India from Sindh and KPK and did not win contested elections in Balochistan. The Siraiki people of today's South Punjab were already in historical conflict with Ranjit Singh's Punjab and were autonomous and sovereign princely territories before the British invasion of Punjab. It was only East Bengal (now Bangladesh), where the AIML was not only founded in 1906, but also won the elections later on in 1946. If the composition of AIML's Central Working Committee (CWC) is reviewed, one finds that only one Sindhi leader M. A. Jinnah was part of it, who in fact resigned from the Indian National Congress (INC) in 1913 due to personal reasons. The rest of AIML's leadership was from Northern India, especially from the pre-partition United Provinces (UP) of India that today form the Utter Pradesh, Bihar and Utrankhand states of India; Delhi, Punjab (today Indian Punjab), the Central Provinces (CP) comprising today's Madhya Pardesh and Andhra Pardesh states, and the East Bengal. There was no Baloch or Pashtun member of AIML's CWC.

Pakistan was demanded by the population and leadership of the undivided Indian provinces / states that today do not form Pakistan. Since Sindhi, Baloch, Pashtun and Siraiki Muslims formed majorities in their historical motherlands; their interests were secure and almost unchallenged within undivided India. Pakistan was demanded by the Muslim minority population and their aristocrat leadership from UP, CP and today's Indian Punjab. Therefore, the creation of Pakistan by clubbing together states that were against the very idea of Pakistan was a historical blunder committed by the colonial British rulers against the will of the people.

After Indian partition in 1947, the state of Pakistan was taken over by those who migrated from Muslim minority provinces of undivided India and settled into newly formed Pakistan. Thus, the non-indigenous peoples' control of the state apparatus transformed the Pakistani state into an anti-indigenous people, particularly against the interests of indigenous ethnic-nations. Like today, the Indian power historically has been led by the northern India. No historical document narrates the movements and struggles by the South Indian people of undivided India. Hence, the partition of India was not only against the will of the federating provinces of today's Pakistan but also did not include the consultation and opinion of the South Indian provinces. It is therefore logically reached that the partition of India was a result of the conflict between northern Indian Muslims, who were aristocrat, and Hindu, who were industrialists and traders over the political and economic power; however the conflict was mostly fostered by the British colonialism to prolong their rule in India.

The extreme-communal mindset of AIML leadership at the time of partition was worth notable especially from the case of Punjabi Sikh community. When the question of Punjab partition arose, the Sikhs were asked to choose between India and Pakistan. They preferred unity of Punjab, and for achieving that they were ready to live in either country for the sake of it. They also considered the option of Pakistan, according to historical documents, because the birth place of their religious messenger Guru Nanak was falling in the proposed Pakistani parts of Punjab; however the AIML leadership rejected the very notion of housing non-Muslims into the land of Muslims. The division of Punjab was painful for Sikh at the time of partition; however the history of victimization of religious minorities in Pakistan have given them a feeling of security and prosperous in India.

Hindu Maha Sabha, Sindh League, Sindh United Party, Unionist Party of Punjab, Sindh Sagar Party, Hur Jam'at (Sindhi), Azad Hind Army, NWFP Congress and Parliament of the autonomous Balochistan were against the partition of India. Rest of the Indian political parties including Communist Party of India as well as the top communist ideologue and philosopher M. N. Roy, an Asian member of Communist International (CommIntern) were also in the favour of Indian partition since.

Sovereign Sindh and Balochistan

Sindh and Balochistan have thousands years history of sovereign countries. They together have also remained one country in the earlier part of their history as a Kingdom of Sindh; however later on they became separate independent and sovereign countries of Sindh and Khanate of Kalat (Balochistan). British invaded sovereign Sindh in 1843 and Balochistan and 1854 in bid to invade Afghanistan. Before their invasion of Sindh-Balochistan, more than a dozen treaties were signed between sovereign country of Sindh and the Great Britain as well as at least one major treaty was signed between the sovereign country of Khanate of Kalat and the Great Britain. According to these treaties, Britain ensured Sindh and Balochistan that it would not invade them; rather protect them, if both open-up river Indus and the route to Kandahar in Afghanistan. British violated its own treaties twice – once when it occupied both by the mid eighties and later in 1947 (Sindh) and 1948 (Balochistan) when both were annexed to Pakistan against the will of the people. British also held treaties with the Siraiki sovereign state of Bahwalpur in 1833 ensuring them protection from the invasion of Ranjit Singh's Punjab. Bahawalpur State and other Siraiki districts, against the sprit of 1833 treaty, were annexed to Pakistani Punjab after 1947.

In fact Sindh waged four wars against British invasion and colonialism in 1843, 1843-1857, 1890-1899 and finally in 1940-1943. In the last war against colonial rule, at least twenty thousand Sindhi combatants, known as Hurs, were killed by British Army and Air Force, and thousands of Sindhi families were sent to concentration camps in Sindh, Rajasthan and Bengal. The freedom war leader Pir Pagara Soriyah Badshah was hanged and his burial place was concealed, which still stands unknown to the Sindhi people. Some Sindhi freedom fighters and guerrilla commanders were hanged, and a large number of them were kept in prisons of Pakistan by the Pakistani authorities until 1965, even after the eighteen years of British departure from Indian Subcontinent.

UK and internal colonialism in Pakistan

Although British departed from Indian Subcontinent (India, Pakistan and Bangladesh) in 1947, it kept its strategic strings attached with Pakistani establishment. United States of America (USA) partnered with Pakistan later on. Pakistan, which was created on the basis of so-called two-nation theory of Indian Muslim-nationhood, broke-up in 1971 on the lines of Bengali ethnic-nationhood after the military committed heinous crimes against humanity of killing and raping hundreds of thousands Bengalis. Pakistan authorities were not even appropriately criticized by the international community against such a brutality. The 1971 break-up of Pakistan on the basis of ethno-national grounds invalidated the 'Two-nation theory' and thus shaken the ideological basis of Pakistan on which it was created by the Britain.

The British connections with the Punjabi dominated Pakistani establishment, partnered by the Urdu speaking northern Indian refugees in Sindh are still of great importance. This is phenomenal from the fact that the largest outward migrations from Pakistan have been of ethnic Punjabi, majority of which have preferred to settle into previous British colonies as well dominion states especially UK, Canada and Australia. Punjabi, particularly Muslim Punjabi, forms significant immigrated population of UK, and are the majority of Vanccour in Canada. The current Governor of Punjab in Pakistan, Muhammad Sarwar, was the first generation immigrant Punjabi who did not only become a Parliamentarian in UK but also was the Deputy Leader of the House in Scottish Parliament. He has migrated back to Pakistan in 2013 after resigning his Parliamentarian seat in UK and became Governor of Punjab within one month of settling back in Pakistan. Despite the fact that ethnic Sindhi are the largest *Southasia*n contributors of the UK economy, they have never remained on the priority of British engagement within Pakistan. Even the non-indigenous leadership of the racial political group like MQM from Pakistan has been given support in UK, who still seems to be stuck on the division of Sindh.

During the sixty-seven years partnership of UK and US in Pakistan, especially their engagement in Afghanistan in the proxy war against USSR, both have been favouring Punjabis and strengthened Punjabi dominated Pakistan Army on the cost of ethnic-nations Sindhi, Baloch, Pashtun and Siraiki.

Sindh is the largest economic contributor of Pakistan. Balochistan and Sindh together form the natural resource richest belt in *Southasia*. Pakistani establishment that is pre-dominantly Punjabi has developed Punjab and Punjabi dominated military on the resources as well as at the cost of Sindh and Balochistan. Thousands have been killed in both of the provinces in last three decades by the armed forces. A highly massive freedom movement is going on in Sindh, which gathered more than five million Sindhis in Karachi on March 23, 2014 and demanded the international community's intervention for the freedom of Sindh.

There is also an armed struggle in Sindh; however it has never attacked a human target. Meanwhile, Baloch are waging a full scale freedom war in Balochistan since 1999 against the occupation of Punjab. Crimes against humanity, genocides and ethnic cleansing have alarmed the people of conscience around the globe.

Possible role of the UK

UK, being successor of the Great Britain, is historically responsible for the ill-designs and mishaps it has committed while departing from the colonies after the Second World War. It should feel more responsible to the oppressed nations in Pakistan whom British invaded as independent and sovereign countries and later on annexed them with the Pakistan against their will. British should also revise its policies and engagement within Pakistan and think undoing the blunders it has committed during 1947 and later on, whose cost is being paid by the Sindhi, Baloch, Pashtun and Siraiki people in Pakistan.

Published in daily Afghanistan Times on September 17, 2014

7
DECOLONISING DEVELOPMENT

The politics of international development has never asserted its hitherto potential role to address changes in development paradigms, rights regimes and social movements in internally colonised countries across the globe. Pakistan, in this regard, could be the first-ever model for this kind of a new initiative.

What role can developed countries like the United States, the United Kingdom and Canada together possibly play in some crucial issues of Pakistan? One may probably dismiss the very notion by terming it irrelevant; however, realpolitik sometimes precedes the theoretical matrix. In fact, the politics of international development has much to offer for development decolonisation in internally colonised countries.

The US, UK, and Canada indeed have a highly peculiar and candid engagement with Pakistan due to various reasons. They are allies in the Afghanistan intervention. They headquarter a highly vibrant Christian missionary in the Punjab and Sindh provinces. Additionally, they house powerful Pakistani Punjabi elite in cities like Vancouver, London and Staten Island in New York. These three cities have played a major role in lobbying for Pakistan's Punjabi-dominated military establishment. Very

few within and outside of Pakistan know the crucially important, diplomatic role these cities have due their degree of influence in Pakistan's internal politics. The US, UK, and Canada are among the top five donors in the development and rights regime in Pakistan, where the largest amount of civil society actors is outcome of, as well as associated with, CIDA, DFID and USAID.

Opposites in similarities

If a wider range of socio-political and strategic facts is taken into account regarding the American, Britain and Canadian niche for economic and financial assistance in Pakistan, the restructuring of such an intervention on ethno-demographic segregation becomes an inevitable prerequisite. This will ultimately have highly progressive effects if other stakeholders like Germany, Russia, India and Japan join in such a noble task.

In the wider range of global politics, Canada hitherto has postured itself as a soft ally of the US and the UK has been an old ally since the Cold War. The UK is a previous coloniser who morally holds greater responsibilities for whatever is happening in Pakistan due its inappropriate and haphazard departure from Pakistan. Moreover, the nature of relations between Canada, US, and the UK as well as the Canadian passion for an enhanced role in global politics further pitches her for revisiting the Pakistan policy.

From the immigration-demographic standpoint, these countries have two edges for their possible role regarding the much required 180-degree reform in Pakistan. Moreover, the UK and Canada have classical similarities as well concerning the dissent between states and the federal government. In the UK, Scotland has its own currency—the Scottish Pound—and a referendum for its cessation is already due. Meanwhile Canada has been appropriately addressing the issue of Quebec, for which they held a referendum. Unlike the UK and Canada, Pakistan has been unsuccessful in addressing similar popular demands from Sindh and Balochistan in a democratic and judicious manner. In fact, these freedom movements in Pakistan have been unfortunately handled through a brutal, undemocratic and unethical use of military power against the citizenry.

The United Kingdom, Canada, and the US house some of the largest populations of Pakistani Punjabis; thus, it becomes relevant for their foreign policies to include the chemistry change in the Pakistani power matrix and statecraft through development intervention policies.

Non-inclusive matrix

There can be a strong role for the US, UK, and Canada in overhauling Pakistan statecraft in association with some Western and *Southasian* stakeholders for the country's real substantive democratisation, which may leave positive impacts on the desperately required state chemistry change. It is now a well-discussed fact among analysts that the state apparatus of Pakistan is non-inclusive unto its very foundations by being confined only to the ethnic Punjabis, mostly of Salafi Muslim origin. The rest of the citizens, especially the Sindhis and Balochs and religious groups like Hindus, Christians and Shia Muslims, are officially or traditionally barred from strategic positions, like the heads of the armed forces. Additionally, non-Muslims are constitutionally discriminated against by being denied their right to hold the public offices of the President and the Prime Minister.

Although there is no constitutional bar on Sindhis and Balochs for the top positions, the practical norms are otherwise. No Sindhi military official has so far been promoted to the post of Brigadier General. Moreover, only one Baloch general has hitherto succeeded to the senior rank who, during Musharaf's military regime, also qualified for the post of Deputy Army Chief. However, he was asked to retire prematurely .

Quite surprisingly, for civil society organisations, international development funds flow, and private entrepreneur recruitment, including for multi-national companies, usually practice ethnic bias in Pakistan because the majority of these house ethnic Punjabi employees in senior and mid-level management. Even in the oil and gas-rich province of Sindh, hardly any Sindhi can be found in technical and non-technical positions for officers and labourers.

Federative dissent

Due to the *Punjabisation* of the state apparatus in Pakistan, in association with its Urdu-speaking elite partners, Bangladesh waged and won a war for freedom in 1971. Balochistan has been waging a liberation war for the last couple of decades and Sindh is leading a peaceful movement where a couple of million people demanded independence in 2012. Recently around five million Sindhis gathered in the Karachi city on March 23, 2014 to demand that the United Nations and the world community intervene for an 'Independent Sindh'. At least two top leaders, Bashir Qureshi and Maqsood Qureshi, have been killed in Sindh during the last two years, besides the extra-judicial murder of hundreds of Sindhi and Baloch political and human rights activists and journalists. More than 10,000 activists, roughly estimating, were involuntarily disappeared from both the southern coastal and natural resource rich provinces of Sindh and Balochistan. Recently, numerous mass graves have been found, according to news reports from various parts of Balochistan, indicating war crimes committed during the conflict between the military and the Baloch rebels.

A crucial engagement

While *Southasia*n countries need to be concerned about happenings in their immediate neighbourhood, developed countries like the US, Canada, the UK, Russia and Japan can play at least one basic yet crucial three-pronged role in Pakistan. One, they can review their foreign policy and international development priorities in the socio-political context and prioritise issues like 'ethno-sectarian participation' in governance as well as human rights support in the context of political, economic and culture rights to Sindh and Balochistan provinces. Two, they can push Pakistan along with other stakeholders to hold a referendum in a democratic manner in Sindh and Balochistan, similar to Canada and the UK's plans to do so in Quebec and Scotland, respectively. Three, where Punjabi-speaking Pakistani settlers in the US, UK and Canada have played a major role in Islamabad's politics and diplomacy, the time has come for the American, Canadian and British Sindhi and Baloch Diaspora to also be encouraged for a progressive role in the state chemistry and a rights regime change in Pakistan. Most importantly, native Western activists can at least show their activism sympathy for the victims of ethnic cleansing, genocide and rights violation in Sindh and Balochistan.

Let development equality be reinforced to strengthen social justice and peace for a better tomorrow.

Published in Daily The Kathmandu Post, Nepal on May 4, 2014

8
COLONIZED INTERNALLY

The boom of socialist politics in the global order between 1950-1970s, the Cold War episode that played out in Afghanistan during the 1980s and the 'war on terror' during the 2000s have been instrumental in state development, social progress, economic growth and the political narrative of Southasia. These global conflicts for power and resources have always been an external factor behind the gap in between states and societies.

After the British withdrawal, Southasian states needed a new state apparatus as the old ones were built to serve the interests of external colonisers. But the continuation of the colonial legacy of the state apparatus created local and internal colonisers who preferred to collaborate with external post-colonial and neo-colonial elements instead of redirecting progress and development to the people.

Due to the much-touted contest between the so-called socialist and capitalist blocks during the 1950-80s, the governments in India, Pakistan, Sri Lanka, Myanmar, Nepal, Bhutan and the Maldives could not bridge the gaps between the state and society by transforming the colonial, aristocratic and monarchical natures of their respective state oligarchies into a localised one.

Internal colonisation

In some of the previous colonies in Asia and Africa, the withdrawal of colonisers created an ethno-linguistic, racial, and/or sectarian hegemony and oligarchy over the rest of the citizenry, especially by transferring state powers to selective or loyal ethno-linguistic and religious groups. South Africa, Indonesia and Pakistan have been typical examples of this.

A federation of previously sovereign and independent countries, Pakistan is a typical case study for internally colonised states. State formation in Pakistan has been a classic hegemony of ethnic Punjabis in association with the cultural, political and economic partnership of the

Urdu-speaking elite over the rest of the federated provinces. Due to the *Punjabisation* of Pakistan's military, civil, non-governmental and non-state elements of power, East Pakistan waged a freedom war and emerged as Bangladesh on the world map.

The Pakistani state had tried to accommodate a thin margin of Pashtuns in anti-Soviet campaigns with the support of the US. And it has internally colonised Sindh and Balochistan by accommodating the Urdu ethnic minority in Karachi city. This has resulted in a popular liberation movement, a low intensity insurgency in Sindh and highly intense warfare in Balochistan provinces. It is worth mentioning here that Sindh is the richest land in Southasia in terms of natural resources like oil, coal and methane gas.

Contemporary discontent

Globalisation has attached virtual wings to the state apparatus across the globe to fly uninterrupted in comparison to society. It has undermined the previous discourse of the gradual reduction in the role of state in societal affairs.

Technological advancements associated with global connectivity have limited the domain of individual liberties, privacy and movements within and across the nation-states. The worst impact of today's state-oriented globalisation, in association with the globalised security doctrines and practices combined with the widening state-society gap, has been pushing the previous colonies to choose between orderly anarchy and result-oriented social movements and transformation.

In fact, the state structures in the previous colonies have become extra-ordinarily advanced and globalised in comparison to their own societies. This phenomenon is exclusive in locally-colonised federations, where federating states/provinces and their ethnic-nations are at odds with the centre or the dominant ethnic groups.

The technology transfer to Pakistan by the West during the last four decades has been misused for the ethnic cleansing of Sindhis and Balochs. The recent unearthing of mass graves in Balochistan and extra-judicial killings in Sindh by security agencies are highly visible evidences of such misuse. It is roughly estimated that the state, as well as state-sponsored mullahs and urban terrorists, have killed around 50,000 commoners so far in Sindh and Balochistan since 2000.

Global linkages

The states of the previous colonies are becoming highly intolerant of social movements, overall rights regimes and individual liberties. The persecution of human rights activists and journalists, the censorship of movies and books, disallowing urban life, limiting freedom for women, attempting to accommodate social movements through structural transformation into failed models are some of the most notable examples. The worst situation can be observed in internally-colonised federations like Pakistan.

Since the people of these countries are in a dilemma of a peculiar kind, in which previous colonisers and neo-imperialists have played key roles, it is necessary that the people from previous colonial and neo-colonial powers come together to raise issues of common concern.

Perversion, dictatorships, local colonies and unnecessary interference of the state apparatus in societies have wrecked havoc in countries like Pakistan.

The time has come for the people of Commonwealth states, of the US and Europe in particular, to step up for real liberation and the development of people in the previous colonies so that states are kept in legitimate brackets, like in countries such as Pakistan.

It is strange that social movements, political rights and civil liberties of the developed and global north societies are highly dependent on the liberation and political salvation of societies in the previous colonies and the Global South. Let the people of previous colonies, particularly internal colonies like Sindh and Balochistan be given moral support in their battle for justice. Proper understanding, will and passion is all that is required to create connectivity for the collectivism of efforts to promote justice.

Besides, studies concerning social movements and civil liberties also need to focus on the process of social-waves versus the structurisation of human institutions. No phenomena in the human history of social progress and spiritual development combined with the relation between 'Being' (man) and 'Absolute Being' (nature) have surpassed this fundamental dynamics of human development.

Let us work out the dialectics of humanism for a better harvest of global citizenry, including poor classes and nations in chains around the world.

Published in Daily The Kathmandu Post, Nepal on March 30, 2014

9
OF STATE AND SOCIETY

Human society has two inherent permanent features and tendencies—
the emergence of social-waves and the process of structuralisation in those
social-waves. This opposition is a chain of causalities, containing the
manifestation of dynamics in the political economy and social progress, as
well as their retrogression and social stagnation. No phenomenon of social
movements around the globe, particularly in the previous colonies, is an
exception to this dialectic of mass expression.

State vs. society

Human history has witnessed and undergone this process through the
structuralisation of movements, religions, ideologies and revolutions. It has
left long-lasting imprints on social institutions, particularly the mega-social
organism of the state, and on the process of state building and state
formation.

The contemporary crises of state versus society and the liberty of the
individual versus the state's reckless vigilance using the excuse of national
security have deep roots in this fundamental dynamic and dialectic of
broader social behavior.

The widening gap between states and societies during the process of
globalisation is at a highly naïve stage in developed countries, if compared
with the developing and underdeveloped world. In other words, state-
society frictions in the global north and south have not only their own
peculiarities but also variant degrees and velocities of social processes. This
is further visible in the polar opposite nature of statehood between the
previous colonies and their colonisers.

Besides, on the debris of the state apparatus in previous colonies and
colonisers, there have emerged the contemporary virtual forms of soft-
colonisation, which no doubt is at the height of neo-colonialism and semi-

34

colonialism. This has highly peculiar connotations in ethno-linguistically diverse societies, countries and their arc of class-cum-federal structures.

The impacts of colonisation on the polity, state-building and state-society relations in previous colonies and their colonisers are evident. Today's virtual colonialism has even worse aspects to this. Thus, the understanding of state-society relations in the global south, particularly in the previous colonies, in the perspective of contemporary politics and social movement would lead to another stage of discourse. Nevertheless, an analysis of the contemporary state-society relations would hardly re-direct to the hidden depths if the '*Structuralism*' versus 'social-wave' dynamics is not at the core of broader discourse.

Almost all religions, practical manifestations of political doctrines, movements, and cultural ethos become dogma once swamped in structuralisation. The institutions of mullahism, priesthood and panditism, political leadership cults, party dictatorship and thinking stereotypes are common examples.

Colonial state formation

State building and state formation are two different aspects of statehood. State building is a process in which the state evolves out of society through gradual evolution whilst state formation is a process where state construction takes place in a non-traditional manner, based mostly on an extraordinary centralised statehood. State formation in most cases involves the role of external factors in the embryology of the state apparatus.

In the process of state formation, peculiar courses of political actions take place, where particular state elements acquire bigger roles or powers (non-traditionally, if not abnormally) in comparison with others in statecraft.

The formation of a colonial state has historically been aimed at providing a buffer between the colonisers and their subjects. This was attained through creating a class of bureaucrats, sallariat (salaried middle class) and the establishment of various forms of rural-lordships.

The contribution of colonisers in terms of political discourse and culture has helped colonial societies to grow. However, it has meant to regulate relations between colonisers and colonies, mostly in the coloniser's interest. This led, for example, to the previous British colonies wearing a new sociality—a reversal of the previous socio-economic relations. Undivided India is a highly intelligible model of studies for that. India underwent social engineering by the British Raj, which created permanent frictions and upheavals, despite the fact that these are at the heart of development dynamics in *Southasia*.

The legacy of colonialism has sprung a new course of socio-political metabolism. The independence of colonies, therefore, have gradually and continuously undergone the process of the post-colonial state versus society, the neo-colonial state versus society and internal-colonial or semi-colonial state versus native or internal semi-colonies.

Freedom and the state

If post-British withdrawal from Southasia is deeply analysed, it will show a peculiar course of state-formation, social progress and consequently, state society conflicts.

If seen in the post-British withdrawal context, various states have undergone an exclusive path to contain the state's classical role of maintaining minimum civil conditions for the citizenry to avail of a free and peaceful life. In so many manners, the state's legitimacy over the use of violence has either been over-used, as in Myanmar and Sri Lanka, or this legitimacy has been shared with state-sponsored extremists, as with the urban terrorists in Pakistan.

The exclusive takeover of the polity and the state apparatus by the particular classes of India after 1947 still carries the strings of colonial statehood, if seen in a state-society perspective. Pakistan has undergone an uneven course of militarisation of the state as well as some selective societal groups. Sri Lanka has taken various courses of state retrogression in which state-society relations have been antagonised through a repressive order where harmony has been compromised over the prioritisation of the ethnic interest between the Tamil and Sinhala people.

Besides, the state has translated itself gradually into militarisation, where minimum civil conditions have always been at the stake. Even Nepal, always proud for never being colonised, has remained under a virtual colonial status since the British occupation of India. Myanmar has become the worst example of a military's dominance over the state apparatus, which turned society retrogressive. Bhutan, like Nepal, is facing the drawbacks of being a land-locked geo-political entity. Maldives, and to certain extent Nepal and Bhutan, has turned itself into a state of convenience in terms of its foreign policy, which ultimately has fall-outs in its own societies and the interests of friendly neighbours. Bangladesh, unlike others, has started cleansing house to detach the impacts, adversaries and strings of Muslim terrorism and war crimes committed by Pakistan in 1971.

Southasian states, naturally, underwent the process of transition after independence from British rule. The state apparatus left behind by the British as an institutional legacy was not only a Southasian adaptation of the Western statehood of its time but was also structured to serve colonial interests and prolong colonial rule. The unexpected withdrawal of the

British from Southasia due to World War II left no room to transform the nature of the state apparatus from colonisation into a real republic.

The states in Southasia are still structured to serve global powers, in comparison with the interests of their own citizens. In the absence of 'real' colonisers, the role of colonisers has been taken over by civil and military elites. This has squared the level of alienation among the people vis-à-vis the state.

Since most Southasian countries constitute a united diversity, they are reluctant for social movements that lead to a transformation of the state and for the judicious distribution of power vertically and horizontally. Empowerment and development in Southasia is, therefore, conditioned on the judicious distribution of power among ethnicities, classes, communities and sects. Besides, the coloniser's leftover state apparatus legacy is the major reason behind the unending conflicts, underdevelopment and militarisation in the region.

If summed up, the transition of Southasian states from colonial into postcolonial states, neo-colonial arrangements and semi-colonial as well as internal colonial states has always been the fault on which politics and development in Southasia has been directed and redirected through certain classes, portions of the states apparatus, elitist mindset and structural cultures of the state-society dynamics.

Published in daily The Kathmandu Post on March 16, 2014

10
ETHNICITY AND URBANIZATION

The transformation of *Southasia* from feudal and rural relations into the urban has enormous development contours along with highly sensitive challenges of its ethno-political stability and governance. Therefore, any discourse focusing cities in *Southasia* cannot avoid the issues and relation between demography, governance, and ethnic stability.

Mega transformation

Southasia amid uncontrolled population growth will have 1.2 billion urban mass by 2050, which no doubt will be the largest urbanisation of human history in any single regional entity. It will be a chain-process of transformation, converting a large number of small into big villages, towns into tertiary cities, and existing small cities into the secondary cities. Today's metropolitans will touch their vertical and horizontal heights. The issues of land, population pressure, demography, resources, and governance as well as the niche of harmonised topography and ethnography will be the major focus for the governments.

This process is bound to change the contours of human settlement and development patterns. The change in sociological configuration due to this has already become visible in some countries, where an increasing number of rural and newly born middle class has started attaining power-opportunities in the societies. Secondary cities augment rural development and play the role of sanctuaries of urbanisation and help creating new middle class and urban poor; thereby filtering the migrations towards metropolitans.

The situation has further strengthened the fold of broader civil society actors in the region that have started ascertaining their role in the given domains. It is expected that the cities like Delhi, Bangalore, and Lahore will cross their status of second line metropolitans in the upcoming decades.

Kathmandu city can also be considered in the queue given the demographic mass and development in Nepal. It is therefore important for the future governance of these cities that the repercussions of uneven development, unplanned urbanisation, and fallouts of existing metropolitans should be taken into the consideration.

Ethnicity and conflicts

Population movement has already altered the socio-economic and demographic structure of the cities in the region and will certainly affect it in future. It has already created in some cases deep issues of ethnic conflict, development disparity, and the contest over resource, which also has resulted into violence sometimes. In Asia, such complex example of urbanisation based on ethnic diversity and antagonism rooted into the migrations is Jakarta. The other examples are Karachi and to certain extent Bangalore. Karachi is a peculiar case study for the region, where ethno-linguistically non-local migrant minority rules the city in terms of electoral politics as well as use of violence; and legislatively resists the urbanisation of native and indigenous Sindhi majority so as their minority rule remain unchallenged.

From the perspective of the growth of urban centres, it is apparent that "net internal migration from rural areas" has played a substantial role in urbanisation. According to UN modulated projections, Pakistan's 48.9 percent population will be living in the urban hubs by 2030.

Karachi has a jerky demographic history. Until 1965, it was a Sindhi majority city, in latter two decades it observed a win-win balance between Sindhi-Balochi, Urdu, and Pashtu ethnic groups. Today, it is again Sindhi-cum-Baloch majority city; however politically ethno-linguist Urdu minority of the city rules it. The city has observed around four waves of violence since 1972, which have taken lives of beyond ten thousand citizens.

Governance, demography and discrimination

Six major demographic groups form the politics of ethnic interests in Karachi. Their population-wise sequence would be indigenous Sindhi and Baloch; Urdu and Bihari, Pashtun and Punjabi migrants; indigenous miscellaneous group of naturalised Parsies, Rajasthanis, and illegal migrants and refugees from Afghanistan, Myanmar, Bangladesh and Iran. The peculiar aspect of this ethnic politics is the contest over the resources and opportunities, in which Urdu speaking Muhajir minority rules not only the city but also Sindh province in many ways.

In Karachi, the ethnic minority through ethnically biased governance and legislation is discriminating the development of indigenous people. During the rule of General Musharaf, the electoral constituencies of Sindh were altered in a manner that the indigenous majority may win lesser seats in the provincial and federal legislature.

Recently, the legislation over a controversial and popularly rejected Sindh Local Government Act has stirred up an insurgency like situation. The Act administratively separates Karachi from rest of the province and the Mayor of the city is given more authorities then the Chief Minister of Sindh. It has at least three discriminative aspects. By administratively converting five districts of Karachi into one, it will give edge to ethno-linguistic Urdu speaking minority, which is the absolute majority in only one district, Central Karachi. The Act gives authorities to the Mayor to decree demolishing of a house or a settlement. This has resulted into demolishing of two historical Sindhi Hindus settlements of Karachi within two weeks of its legislation in October 2012. The other ethnic groups of the city fear that this authority would be used against Sindhi, Baloch, Pashtun and Punjabi settlements, which together form nearly 70 percent of the metropolitan.

Lessons for the Southasia

The ongoing urbanisation in *Southasia* is bound to create ethnic diversity in the existing and emerging cities; therefore, if this aspect is not part of urban planning, the ethnic chaos is inevitable. Avoiding urban conflicts, the right to rule and opportunities needs to be ensured to the ethnic indigenous population.

The urbanisation in *Southasia* will also be carrying along the issues like poor governance, limited resources, housing, non-futuristic planning; infrastructure inadequacy; transportation lethargy and environmental problems. This requires adopting modern frameworks of urban planning, comprehensive master plans, efficient land-use, and appropriate zone regularization as well as building control. The future of *Southasian* cities could only be save through non-traditional and futuristic vision and planning that does not compromise rights of the land, native population as well as city dwellers.

Published in Daily The Kathmandu Post on November 24, 2012

11
TOWARDS ONE SOUTHASIA

Pakistani Prime Minister Nawaz Sharif, like ex-president Asif Ali Zardari, has recently tuned up the good old mantra of a visa-free India-Pakistan. However, the nature of geopolitical relations between these two countries alone is the major hurdle to a visa-free regime in the region. Given the fact that visa arrangements and norms between the rest of the Southasian countries are almost on the verge of border-free regional entities, it is speculated that a visa-and-border-free Southasia can only be realised, unlike the European Union, through a gradual visa-and-border regime change.

Southasian contours

Since Pakistani state behaviour towards India has been of an infiltrative and offensive mode when it comes to peace and security, the reaction from India has been inevitable, although mild most of the time. It is therefore necessary to envision a paradigm shift in the Southasian visa regime, particularly between India and Pakistan. This requires out-of-the-box thinking around state apparatus, ethnic diversity, economic stability, demographic sovereignty and security, as well as the handling of intra-state conflicts, which in most countries has remained militaristic.

Nepal is still struggling to shape an appropriate statehood. Sri Lanka has yet to build a social contract between the Sinhala and Tamil people. Bhutan has to think on the violence around Buddhism. India has to deepen its federal practices by addressing issues in Kashmir as well as in its north-eastern parts. Pakistan has to alter the web of statehood, federalism and dismantle ethnic Punjabi hegemony on Sindh, Balochistan and Khyber Pakhtunkhuwa.

Pakistan, by all aspects, is not only a peculiar state in Southasia but also a must review case study among the federations of the globe, where ethno-sectarian monotony, ethnically exclusive statehood and state ideology stereotype has turned Pakistan into steadily failing state.

Dismantling the hexagon

Pakistan is the only country in the region whose internal politics and state fault lines are casting a shadow of instability, not only in South and Central Asia but around the globe too. Pakistan, thus, is badly affecting the neighbourhood through its hexagonal state chemistry and characteristic. The *'Punjabisation'* of the state apparatus; cultural *'Urduisation'*; non-indigenous takeover of the deep-state (by the 1947 refugees of Punjabi, Urdu and Kashmiri origin); dominancy of the ethno-linguistic Punjabi minority on the rest; imposition of the sectarian Wahabi-Salafi Muslim minority over the rest of the Muslims, Hindus and Christians; and finally, the militarisation of almost all state and non-state apparatus is the hexagonal statehood that is causing instability in Southasia and state failure in Pakistan.

Averting state-failure as well as ensuring peace, stability and security in Southasia depends on dismantling these hexagonal bonds in the state molecules of Pakistan. This ultimately means drastic reforms and paradigm shift in the state, society, and politics of Pakistan.

The primary task for avoiding the possible break-up of Pakistan and ensuring stability, peace, and Southasian regionalisation is to fulfil the fundamental task of electing a Constituent Assembly (CA) for the first time in the history of Pakistan. The CA should have a mandate to legislate and regularise ethnic balance in the armed forces and security agencies based on the proportionate participation of Sindhi, Punjabi, Baloch, Pashtun, Siraiki, Hindko, Balti and Urdu speaking Sindhis; guarantee the indigenous majority's demographic sovereignty in their historical provinces; the separation of religion from the state; banning violent Madaris; change in the nomenclature as well as legislative authority of the 'Provincial Assemblies' into 'Legislative State Assemblies'; and abolishing the bar on Hindus, Christians and Ahmadiyas for holding the offices of the President, Prime Minister, chiefs of the armed forces and security agencies. Restricting the role of military to border defence and change in state-ideology from a two nation theory into an Indus nationhood would be a step forward. Pakistan being renamed a Union of Indus States would certainly change the course of Southasian polity and equity. If the institution of the President is continued, the governors of the provinces/states should be elected through the Provincial Legislative Assemblies, whilst the institution of the Presidency should be made ceremonious.

If these very basic reforms are not made, the emergence of Sindh and Balochistan as sovereign countries can become inevitable. Prime Minister

Sharif, if willing, can perform this noble job during his term or even after completing his five years tenure.

Neighbourly learning

Pakistan in fact needs to adopt the better federal practices of other neighbour countries, for example India, which on the demand of Tamil Nadu state, recently sent a Foreign Minister to the Commonwealth meeting of state-heads in Sri Lanka. Likewise, a refugee's adoption here also needs the consent of the state (provincial) government where the refugee intends to settle. Besides, a Prime Minister in India resolves major issues through joint online conference with the Chief Ministers and the cabinet. Moreover, barrage land, which is precious in the arid desert of Rajasthan, cannot normally be purchased by the first generation of internal migrants from other Indian states. Similarly, a non-Kashmiri usually cannot be a caretaker of a Hindu temple in Kashmir. None can be a minister in another state, unlike Pakistan where Punjabis and Pashtuns usually become ministers in Sindh; however, such a practice has never been seen in Punjab, Balochistan and Khyber Pakhtunkhuwa provinces.

Road to one Southasia

The demographic composition of Sindh and to certain extent Balochistan is being altered at the behest of the Pakistani establishment, which has adopted British tactics of occupying colonies by shifting its own or friendly populations over to other lands. Punjabi, Afghani Pashtun, Rohangyan Muslim and other Muslim origin refugees from across the world are mostly being settled in Sindh and Balochistan, thus creating demographic insecurities for locals. Besides, a US and Turkish assessment has unveiled that Sindh houses the largest reserves of gas, oil and coal in Southasia. Therefore, Punjab and Urdu speakers are trying to take hold of the province. Amid such a contest over land and natural resources, demographic insecurities and indigenous people's right to rule their historical motherlands, the people of Sindh and Balochistan will never welcome a borderless Southasia and a visa-free India-Pakistan until the federal structure and state chemistry is altered.

Recent developments and the thawing of US-Iran relations will further reduce the strategic importance of Pakistan in Asia, thereby creating an avenue to nullify the clientalism, corporatism and monopoly of the military and its dominating ethnic Punjabis over the rest of Pakistan. Visa-free India-Pakistan is impossible without state as well as federal reforms in Pakistan. One Southasia is not possible without reforms in Pakistan.

Published in Daily The Kathmandu Post, Nepal on December 22, 2013

12
AN OPEN LETTER TO SHEIKH HASINA

We owe you applause, your Excellency Sheikh Hasina Wajid, for your government's significant steps in bringing the perpetrators of war crimes in 1971 to justice. This expression of cheer by a Sindhi in exile is the continuity of an earlier generation of Sindhis and Balochs who shed blood tears over heart-wrecking brutalities, like massacres and rapes, rendered by the Pakistan Army in 1971 in Bangladesh. The political, social, and literary leadership of that time in Sindh and Balochistan in Pakistan was supporting Banglabandhu Sheikh Mujibur Rehman. Hundreds, if not thousands, took to the streets of Sindh cities and towns against the military operation in Bangladesh (then East Pakistan). Although, Sindhis and Balochs themselves are today facing gradual an ethnic cleansing-like situation.

War crimes

Humanity can never forgive those who killed three million civilians and raped hundreds of thousands of innocent women with the support of the military-supported right-wing terrorists of Al-Shams and Al-Badar in Bangladesh, who were outfits of Jamait-e-Islami Pakistan. Unfortunately, these local butchers were ethno-linguistically non-Bengalis of Bihari origin, who were playing the same tune as a Karachi-based party of refugees (Muhajirs) has been playing in Sindh for the last two decades at the behest of Pakistan's security establishment.

It was the political course of 1960s. The Awami League of Sheikh Mujibur Rehman had a relatively strong existence in Sindh after East Pakistan. Both Sindh and East Bengal together fought against the banning of Sindhi and Bengali languages and the introduction of a One-Unit federal mechanism by the military regimes of General Ayub and Yahya Khan. The vote bank of Sindh was divided along the lines of the supporters of Benazir Bhutto and the supporters of Sheikh Mujibur Rehman. Political icons like

G M Sayyed, Qazi Faiz Mohammad and many others were staunch critics of the ethnic Punjabi domination of Pakistan and thus, lost their seats due to rigging engineered by the military regime of General Yahya Khan.

In commemoration

In early 1972, a highly popular Sindhi nationalist-cum-leftist leader Rasool Bux Palijo wrote the first ever book on Bangladesh war crimes and organised a peasant protest in Sindh for the freedom of Sheikh Mujibur Rehman while also demanding action against military officials accused of war crimes. As expected in a militarised country like Pakistan, the Hammod Rehman (Judicial) Commission was constituted to inquire into the war crimes and secession of Bangladesh. However, the commission's crucial findings and observations have not yet been made public and nor has the guilty military leadership been punished.

It is also worth appreciating that your government has bestowed awards to the G M Syyed, Qazi Faiz Ahmed and Anwar Pirzado from Sindh and Ghous Bux Bizanjo from Balochistan for their support of the Bengali people during the 1971 military operation. Although your second lieutenants forgot to include Rasool Bux Palijo in the list, a Lahore-based Punjabi activist-cum-lawyer, who like other Punjabis, kept mum over the war crimes during 1971, has also been given an award.

Similarly, the Punjab-born prominent Urdu progressive poet Faiz Ahmed Faiz was also given an award for his poem 'Hum ke thahrey ajnabi, itni mulaqaton ke baad'. Faiz chose 'Suqot-e-Dhaka' (The Fall of Dhaka) as the title for a poem. But the poem is in fact an expression of grief over the separation of East Pakistan from the West, not a condemnation of war crimes against Bengalis during the eight-month military campaign. Activists, journalists and intellectuals of that era in Pakistan recall when Faiz, who was a retired captain of the army, was interviewed by BBC Radio Urdu Service during the military operation in Bengal. He announced that he would return the Lenin Peace Prize if the Soviet Union did not stop supporting the Bengali secessionists.

To the ICC

Bengal won its freedom from the ethnic monopoly of Punjab. The rest of the people in Pakistan are still undergoing a form of apartheid. Since your government has already started cleaning house, the time has come to take one-step forward. Criminals in the Pakistan military and their cronies in the Pakistani establishment need to be taken to the International Criminal Court (ICC) for their war crimes in Bangladesh. Such an initiative will be true justice for the thousands of civilians killed and raped. This will not only inch Bangladesh towards international justice but also prove to be great support to the oppressed peoples of Sindh, Balochistan and

Pakhtunkhuwa in Pakistan, as well as a long-term bailout for peace and security in Southasia.

There is no iota of possibility for the sustenance of internal social movement to demilitarise Pakistan's polity and society and offer salvation to the people of Sindh and Balochistan from the ethnic hegemony of Punjab. Bangladesh going to the ICC would permanently restrict the Pakistani military from derailing democracy and prevent them from committing crimes against humanity concerning Sindhi, Baloch, Hindu, Christians and Ahmedi people. Moreover, the military would then limit itself to defence affairs and avoid interfering in the political arena of the country. Such a step would be a great contribution to the stability and security of Southasia. Joy Bangla! Joy Sindh! Long live the Indus people!

Published in Daily The Kathmandu Post, Nepal on January 12, 2014

13
PEACE BEYOND KASHMIR

Politics in Pakistan has some basic state-ideological, political morality and country-hood fault lines that, in terms of statecraft, are at the helm of almost all internal political catastrophes as well as regional instabilities.

The basic laws of motion in the dynamics of possible change in Pakistan through the futurological view ultimately depend on the country's external engagements, and vice-versa. Peace and the people's security as well as sovereignty within the fragile Pakistani statehood and in *Southasia* is the greatest concern of our times, especially when this most volatile geo-strategic region houses the nuclear capable Islamic republic, which is sitting on a time bomb of extremism. Pakistan needs to appropriately think, assess and adopt unavoidable political as well as statecraft actions and reforms if it seriously wants to avoid state-failure. The same also applies to its neighbourhood, as allies vis-à-vis their engagement and interests with Pakistan.

Fault lines of political systems

India and Pakistan carried forward colonial political systems after the partition of India in 1947 by continuing with the centralised institution of the Governor General as head of state. However, it was later replaced with the institution of the Presidency. In the context of the political system, the existence of Presidents and Prime Ministers is obvious in countries where the state-society gap—and to a certain extent, antagonism—is highly visible. Nevertheless, positive alterations have also been made; for example in India, by confining Presidencies to ceremonial state leadership. Establishments in previous Asian colonies mostly have the internal security environment of state-society antagonism. It is at this point that the people's security is compromised by non-participatory establishments in the name of the nation-state security paradigm, which prioritises geography over people.

It is only with the presidential form of the governance that state and society attempt to create a point of merger. The continuation of the Governor General's institution in India and Pakistan were evolutionary take offs from the colonial form of statehood, statecraft and polity, even after the departure of British. This is ultimately identical to the separation of state from society, translating itself into the separation between the representatives of the state and that of the people's governance. The institutions of Governor Generals, Presidents and Prime Ministers have bifurcated states and societies into polar opposites. Thus, the establishments of *Southasian* countries have always kept themselves at bay from their own people and societies. This is the major reason, in terms of political philosophy as well as systems, why societies have expressed their symbolic withdrawal from the state through various social movements.

Invasion of Kashmir, 1948

Kashmir has remained a major cause of disagreement in India-Pakistan relations, which has ultimately had adverse effects on peace and human security in all of *Southasia*.

Kashmir became a bone of contention when the Pakistan Army, newly craved out of the Royal Indian Army, attacked Kashmir, which according to the settlement of the Indian Partition was a state of India. There are many existing narratives on that particular war of 1948, which have become a centre of debate for historians. However, no historical narratives of the war mention who ordered and authorised the offensive to invade Kashmir. Jinnah, the Governor General and founder of Pakistan, never gave any such orders to the Pakistan Army. It was the then Chief of Army Staff who in fact started the offensive. This breach of political morality and the fundamental norm of the statecraft had long lasting impacts on the politics of Pakistan as well as peace and security in *Southasia*.

The 1948 Pakistan-India war primarily decided the political future of Pakistan in which the military became the driving force of almost all affairs within and outside the country. Besides, this unauthorised and illegitimate invasion of Kashmir was the core reason behind the six decade-long cold and hot wars between India and Pakistan.

Constitutional illegitimacy

Pakistan was an unexpected and unplanned outcome of the British withdrawal from the subcontinent in 1947. Pakistan had never existed in human history. It was created out of two historically sovereign countries of Sindh and Balochistan and the partition of the Punjab and Pashtun areas from Afghanistan. The country has no politically legitimate constitution since 1947. A couple of constitutions were imposed on the newborn country between 1950 to 1970 by military regimes. Moreover, no Constituent Assembly was elected in 1973 to form the constitution.

The break-up of Pakistan in 1971, in which Bangladesh dislodged the so-called two-nation theory of Hindu and Muslim nations and claimed nation-statehood along ethno-linguistic lines, invalidated the foundations on which Pakistan was created. It was therefore imperative, according to international norms and political morality, that the state of Pakistan would have convened a Constituent Assembly through which the four federating states would have reached a new social contract of living within Pakistan. Unfortunately, the military dominated Pakistan and its ethnic Punjabi supremacy did not consider this option. It is therefore that Pakistan today is facing highly popular and massive freedom movements in Sindh and Balochistan.

Unfolding knots

Pakistan is undergoing greater waves of chaos and anarchy due to unreasonable policies, actions and intentions of the security establishment. The dominance of the military in every sphere of the country; the virtual colonisation of Sindh, Balochistan and Khyber Pakhtunkhuwa by the Punjabi elite; the unwillingness for a new social contract between the federated provinces after the country's break-up in 1971; and the attachment of the state-ego with Kashmir after an unjustified and unauthorised 1948 Kashmir war are core foundations of Pakistan's rouge state behavior.

Pakistan has to dislodge the many unnecessary strings it has attached through its history. Besides, it has to correct internal political legalities and legitimacies, especially in the context of province-province as well as provinces-federation relations. This essentially requires the separation of religion from the state as well as restricting the role of the military to defence, as devised by the political leadership of the country. These internal and external changes are prerequisites for peace and prosperity within Pakistan and consequently, in the *Southasia*. Pakistan has to choose one option out of 'decay or destruction.' The time for the third-way is now over.

Published in Daily The Kathmandu Post on November 24, 2013

14

STATE OF SOVEREIGNTY

The technological inclusion of drones in the global security paradigm as a defensive-offence mechanism has kicked off a new set of discussions and discourse based on a broad range of concerns and questions. Especially in the countries that consider drones a threat to their sovereignty and national security. Besides, drone operations, particularly in Pakistan and Yemen, have also raised the question of their international legality and legitimacy in the context of nation-state sovereignty.

There is a rule of thumb in technological developments within the military-strategic sphere around the globe that technological advancements are balanced out either through counter technological developments or by attaining similar capabilities. The discussion that falls beyond the orbit of this principle is very important in today's globalised politics.

There are essentially three basic aspects to focus on regarding drones and their operations: i) the notion of a nation-state versus regional and international sovereignty; ii) aspects of international laws and globally agreed to norms concerning war, escalation, spying and use of territorial space; and iii) the reality of the positive outcomes of droning versus the two former aspects.

Given the changing perspective of nation-state sovereignty in contemporary global politics and international security, broader reforms are needed in the various treaties, covenants, conventions, procedures and the mandate of the United Nations to redraw limits. Besides, it has become a niche of our time to de-limit international legal and diplomatic taboos from the legal framework perspective, particularly regarding the notion of sovereignty amid sharply strengthening inter-dependent sovereignties among nation-states. It is also essential to reimagine cooperation among national, international and global stakeholders that require the inclusion of security perspectives as an integral part of the international legal framework.

It is highly important to summit around the collectively agreed upon 'exceptionalism' in the foreign policies of world powers like the US, UK, France, Russia, India, China, Germany, Canada and Australia regarding rogue and failed states so that a new wave of global statehood can appropriately come into being. In many cases, new nations need to emerge on the debris of failure. A reshuffle is required to redesign the global world in such a manner that a great number of exiting conflicts are resolved.

The war-peace contours of the world are also changing their meanings. No war can be justified from the sustainable peace perspective; however, war or offence that fulfils globally agreed upon legal frameworks; upholds basic collective rights regimes as well as political morality; ensures international security and is consented to by international forums like the UN are the exceptions. Therefore, if the world community discusses any new legality around drones in the context of international security, it should also consider emerging global interdependency as well as the debate around foreign policy 'exceptionalism' from the global security point of view.

The conflicting aspects of international legal principles versus practical realities are important. The most important case in this perspective is of Pakistan, where droning is termed a violation of the nation-state sovereignty by the government. However, a majority of people think otherwise. Pakistan's stance on droning and the productive outcomes of droning are polar opposites. No doubt droning has proved to be more productive in targeting criminals that fight a dirty war in the name of Islam. The question arises, although violating the territorial and spatial sovereignty of Pakistan, the droning of tribal areas by the US is ensuring the security and sovereignty of the liberal and secular majority in the provinces of Sindh, Balochistan, Khyber Pakhtunkhuwa (KP) and the southern parts of Punjab. In that realm, the sovereignty notions of Pakistan's military dominated security establishment and of the majority people are antagonistic to each other. Therefore, although, violating the international legality of Pakistan's nation-state sovereignty, droning is in favour of people's sovereignty there. This was further validated in August 2013, when a ruling Pakistani Muslim League minister told the parliament that Pakistan would legalise US droning by reaching an agreement, albeit Pakistan itself would use the drones against uprisings within the country (pointing to freedom movements in Sindh and Balochistan). Given the case review of droning in Pakistan, the international community should also consider peoples' sovereignty and the security aspect while agreeing upon any international stance as well as legal frameworks around the use of drones.

Ironically, Pakistan, which is attempting to raise issues of civilian causalities from droning, is itself involved in the murder of thousands of Sindhi and Baloch and to some extent, Pashtun civilians, in the name of the country's so-called internal security. A state that has time and again been implicated in the massive killing of its own citizens is toeing the line of civilian causalities. If the concerned world has to agree to Pakistan's stance on droning regarding civilian causalities, it must also ask Pakistan to stop killing its own people in Sindh and Balochistan.

Finally, droning, which genuinely falls under international security concerns and does not violate the peoples' sovereignty perspective, should be legalised through international legal frameworks for the general good of humanity. However, ensuring zero-sum innocent civilian causalities should become mandatory. The time has come for the international community to create a new international and global legal order and reconsider obsolete diplomatic mechanisms.

Shah, a Pakistan born human rights activist, is an asylum seeker in India. He is the author of Beyond Federalism a political treatise on social movements in Sindh.

Published in Daily The Kathmandu Post on November 3, 2013

15

AFGHANISTAN'S FUTURE DEPENDS ON MAJORITY WILL AND WORLD COOPERATION

The "first world war on Afghanistan" began in 1979 and concluded in 1991, resulting in a decisive defeat of the then-Soviet Union. If seen in the context of people's history, almost 2.802 billion people suffered the direct, indirect and post-direct burns of the Afghan drama in Afghanistan, Pakistan, Iran, China, Uzbekistan, Tajikistan, Azerbaijan and India and later on, post 9/11, in the United States, UK and European Union. If the war and war-related expenditure by the international community in Afghanistan is roughly calculated, it would probably exceed $10 trillion.

Today, the world powers and "stakeholder states" are planning to withdraw from Afghanistan in 2014 in a hasty manner, which ultimately will unfold a new arena of global conflicts and complexities. The process of ISAF (International Security Assistance Force - NATO) withdrawal is the appropriate solution for sustainable power transformation to the Afghan government; however, the post-withdrawal strategy for the substantive peace, development, human security and statehood is the key toward everlasting sustenance of the Afghan sovereignty. Moreover, eventually sustenance comes only through the will and strengthening of leading role of the locals in the statecraft and counterterrorism.

Briefing the Interests

The world has been after Afghanistan at least since the early 18th century because of its strategic location and resource abundance. Rich in minerals including copper, iron-ore, hydrocarbons, gold, lithium, granite, petroleum, natural gas and others, but landlocked amid high mountains with a harsh climate, the country is positioned in the middle of the geopolitical, geo-economic and therefore one of the most geostrategically-important regions of the world.

Afghanistan is the point of common action between and among the international interests like the United States, the UK, Canada, Germany, India, Russia, Australia, China and the Central Asian States. The country can connect Eurasia with the Middle East, South and East Asia, as well as vice versa. At the helm of such a geo-economic reality, Afghanistan has the potential to facilitate the distribution of many hounded energy resources to the global energy corporate sector and thereby, fulfil the energy requirements of world citizenry. The corporate sector of the world has become more globalized today; however, the consumers of the world have not been given the necessary space by the nation-states to become world citizens. No doubt, the commoners of the world will one day also become world citizens in political-economic terms through the process of people's globalization, which is already underway, albeit with a slower evolutionary pace.

If the monetary and financial expenditure of the first and second world wars in Afghanistan is compared with the global monetary requirement for eradicating poverty, terrorism, and death of opportunities for unemployed youth, it reveals the difference, and in many cases antagonism, between contemporary "states" and "statehood" in the contemporary world and the socio-economic, cultural, and spiritual requirements of the citizenry. The phenomena may be termed as "state-deception" when the "security" doctrines by the states conflict with the security opinion of their own citizenry. Thus, states in general today keep a security notion, which is often exclusionary of the people's broader socio-economic, cultural, and spiritual security perspective.

Every country has its own stakes in Afghanistan. Therefore, everyone wants the regional and global politics that tilt to serve their interests. This has become a genuine cause behind the non-consensus over an Afghan solution between and among almost all the countries and regional groups of countries.

On the other hand, Pakistan has been tossing the counterfeit coin of barbaric Taliban, whose interpretation of Islamic Shariah is of the dark ages, against the extraordinary Indian influence and role in the reconstruction of Afghanistan.

Iran was, in fact, fine earlier with NATO forces toppling the Taliban because the Taliban, ethno-linguistically Af-Pak and bordering Pashtun and Punjabi, are upholders of militant *salafisim/Wahabism* and support the involvement in massacres of their Persian-speaking rivals, largely Shia Muslims having historical and cultural affinity with Iran. Taliban also killed more than a dozen Iranian diplomats. Besides, Taliban were supported through Arab-Punjabi nexus in the form of Pakistan-Saudi Arabia-Gulf States trio.

The approach of Iran toward NATO intervention changed later on when there emerged a diplomatic row between the United States and Iran over Iran's nuclear facility. Although the changing internal modes of Iranian polity, with particular focus on internal reforms and foreign policy softness, has created an opportunity for healthier US-Iran engagement. The friendly Iran-American relationship, in association with their already deeper engagement with India, may help support the Afghanistan, Central and *Southasia*n peace spectrum as well as to a certain degree the Middle-East peace process based on an Israel-Palestine resolution. China and the United States are not on the same page on Afghanistan, as China has adopted a highly calculated approach toward Afghan affairs.

According to research by Sandra Destradi, Nadine Godehardt and Alexander Frank, the United States itself is increasingly focused on a region that is referred to as the "Greater Central Asia" or (especially) the idea of a "New Silk Route" initiative. Reviving the old trade routes of the Silk Road has been central to the American discourse.

Canada wants an absolute withdrawal of troops in 2014. Germany and Turkey have been playing the role of catalyst in the engagements between conflicting interests, along with Riyadh and Abu Dhabi, both of whom tow a pro-Taliban line. Amid all these conflicting interests, ISAF withdrawal of 2014 proves to be an issue of concern.

Russia will have to keep a check on formidable economic rivals in Afghanistan like China, according to Monika Pawar, a research student in Delhi, India.

The Costliest War of Our Time

According to the Afghan Study Group, Joseph Stiglitz, the recipient of the 2001 Nobel Prize in economics, and Linda Bilmes, a professor at the Harvard Kennedy School, have said that the direct cost of the Afghan war for the US has already topped $600 billion. Ongoing military operations will bring that total to at least $700 billion through 2014.

According to the research project "Costs of War," by Brown University's Watson Institute for International Studies, the final bill (of the Afghan war for the United States) will run at least $3.7 trillion and could reach as high as $4.4 trillion. The United States is projected to have 32,000 troops in Afghanistan at the end of February 2013, and the US may keep as many as 8,000 to 10,000 troops in advisory and support roles in Afghanistan for some years beyond the withdrawal of combat forces after 2014. James Kirkup in The Telegraph, reports the United States has agreed to pay $2.6 billion per year through 2024 for the Afghan security forces.

According to a Reuters report, 224,000 to 258,000 people have died directly from warfare, including 125,000 civilians in Iraq. An additional 365,000 have been wounded. However, it is assumed that if one counted the death toll due to civic problems created by the wars (the loss of clean drinking water, health care and nutrition), the number would be much higher than that of direct war causalities.

According to James Kirkup's report in The Telegraph, "Afghan operations had cost UK taxpayers a total of £17.3 billion ($28 billion) on top of the core defence budget." With a military engagement of 9500 troops, Britain lost 414 lives until early 2012. It was estimated in the UK that the war would cost it at least another £800 million ($1.2 billion) between 2012 and 2014. (Under severe economic pressure, France also decided to pull back 3,300 troops from Afghanistan.)

Independent estimates are different and according to a report by Richard Norton-Taylor, the war has cost Britain at least £37billion ($60 billion). That means more than £2,000 ($3,200) for every taxpaying household. By 2020, Britain will have spent at least £40 billion on its Afghan campaign, enough to recruit over 5,000 police officers or nurses and pay for them throughout their careers. It could fund free tuition for all students in British higher education for 10 years.

According to initial Canadian government cost estimation for Afghanistan engagement for the period 2001 to 2009, the cost of war was CAD $9 billion, however the CAD $5 billion was added up in the earlier estimated budget in March 2008 due to some equipment purchases. The independent estimates, according to the "Fiscal Impact of the Costs Incurred by the Government of Canada in support of the Mission in Afghanistan" the total cost of the conflict range as high as CAD $18.5 billion by 2011.

Pakistan's civil economy has suffered direct and indirect losses of up to $67.93 billion since 2001. According to the Economic Survey of Pakistan, "Pakistan's investment-to-GDP ratio has declined from 22.5 percent in 2006-07 to 13.4 per cent in 2010-11 with serious consequences for the job creating ability of the economy."

A research paper by Bruck Tillman and others (Tilman Bruck et al, "The economic cost of German participation in Afghanistan war," JPR, Sage Publications, India, May 2013), the German share of the net present value of the total costs of the war ranges from 26 billion Euro to 47 billion Euro. On an annual basis, it is estimated that the German participation in the war costs between 2.5 and 3 billion Euro.

Ian McPhedran, in his report says each soldier out of the 1,550 in Afghanistan is costing Australian taxpayers $1 million. By June 2013, the overall outlay for the Afghanistan campaign will reach more than $7.4 billion, including $1 billion for enhanced measures to better protect soldiers from roadside bombs and rocket attacks.

According to Krupnov, chairman of the Society for Friendship and Co-operation with Afghanistan, Russia would need $50 billion for accelerated industrialization in Afghanistan through 2020. According to Russian experts, the money is needed to launch pipeline transit projects from Turkmenistan to India and from Iran to India via Afghanistan, as well as for the electrification of the country.

Regarding multilateral aid, China has rendered financial aid of RMB 30 million ($5 million), as well as US $1 million, and would further provide Afghanistan with assistance of US $150 million. According to The People's Daily (UN), World Bank and Asian Development Bank estimated during 2001 that at least US $15 billion were needed for Afghanistan's reconstruction. US $10 billion was needed for the first five years alone. In this regard, Japan donated US $500 million, Iran promised US $560 million, Saudi Arabia US $220 million, and EU promised US $495 million. Japan, the second-largest donor of reconstruction and development aid to Afghanistan, is eyeing it for its economic engagement in Central Asia and Afghanistan.

India, being fifth largest donor in Afghanistan, has contributed more than $2 billion for its development. India has already invested US $10.8 billion in Afghanistan as of 2012. More such projects are likely to come up after NATO's withdrawal. Ahead of Afghan President Hamid Karzai's June 2012 visit, according to NDTV, New Delhi cleared $100 million in aid for the third phase of the Small Developmental Projects for Afghanistan as part of its commitment on a $2 billion aid program. The SDPs (Small Development Projects) were earlier implemented in two phases. The first phase, in July 2006, was comprised of 50 projects worth $11,216,179, and the second phase in June 2008 was comprised of 51 projects worth $8,579,537.

Japan would further provide $117 million of direct assistance for development projects in Afghanistan; however, it has already contributed $400 million in the Afghan development initiatives by way of the various UN agencies. Japan is the second largest development donor in Afghanistan, as US stands first. Japan implemented approximately USD $1.6 billion of assistance before 2011.

Despite these initiatives, there is concern among Afghan civil society over the civil-aid deficit, which is based on the expenditure of development initiatives management. Because the key technical consultants, managers, and other assessment staff associated with the projects are employed by the country facilitating support, a large sum of financial reimbursement is sent back to the country supporting aid. According to the Richard Norton-Taylor's report this accounts for 40 percent of the total development aid.

Global Poverty Perspective of the War

According to the International Labour Organization (ILO) report, Global Employment Trends 2012: Preventing a Deeper Jobs Crisis, the world faces the "urgent challenge" of creating 600 million productive jobs over the next decade in to generate sustainable growth and maintain social cohesion. The report mentions the global backlog of 200 million unemployed people and clearly indicates that by the next decade, another 400 million jobs will be required to couch human needs. The world faces the additional challenge of creating decent jobs for the estimated 900 million workers living with their families below the US $2 a day poverty line, mostly in developing countries. It mentions that 74.8 million youth aged 15-24 were unemployed in 2011 around the globe. Indicating the deteriorating world economy, it points out that since 2007, an increase of more than 4 million unemployed people was reported.

In an earlier report (Global Employment Trends 2011: The challenge of a jobs recovery), the ILO mentioned that equally unsettling is the outlook for youth unemployment, which the ILO categorizes as the number of people aged between 15 and 24 who are actively seeking work but unable to find it. There was a slight reduction in youth unemployment last year from 79.6 million to 77.7 million, but the jobless rate for the young still stands at 12.6 percent. "In some countries, the outlook is even worse," it states. "Spain has youth unemployment of 40 percent, while young people in Southeast Asia and the Pacific are 4.7 times more likely to be unemployed as adults. One of the root causes of the revolution in Tunisia was the unrest caused by having a growing number of young people without jobs: the ILO estimates that in North Africa as a whole 'an alarming' 23.6 percent of economically active young people were unemployed in 2010."

A World Bank blog-report on *Southasia* mentions that over a million youth, which forms 21 percent of the population in Britain, are currently out of work. The 'arc of unemployment' cuts across southern Europe through the Middle East to *Southasia*. Almost half of the world's young people live along this arc. *Southasia*n unemployed youth form 31 percent of the global youth population, forming the largest percentage of unemployed youth in the developing world.

The Global Employment Trends for Youth 2013 section of the ILO report mentions that the youth unemployment rate in North Africa is very high, at 23.7 percent in 2012. The unemployment rate for young women is even higher, at 37 percent, compared with 18.3 percent for young men in 2012. The outlook for the coming years remains bleak, with youth unemployment projected to remain close to 24 percent until 2018.

The North African region has by far the highest rate of working poverty, says the aforementioned ILO report, estimated at 40.1 percent in 2012 at the US $1.25 per day level, and working is a necessity for many young people. At the US $2 per day level, the working poverty rate rises to 64 percent; only *Southasia* has a working poverty rate at comparable levels (although the working poverty rate at the US $1.25 per day level is significantly lower in *Southasia*).

According to the fact sheet by The Hunger Project, the world has a population of 7 billion people and 870 million of those people face hunger. Approximately 98 percent of the world's undernourished people live in developing countries. China, India, Pakistan and Bangladesh house 60 percent of the world poor. The region-wise populaces of malnutrition include 578 million in Asia and the Pacific; 239 million in Sub-Saharan Africa; and 53 million in Latin America and the Caribbean. Approximately 60 percent out of them are women. Malnutrition is the key factor contributing to more than one-third of all global child deaths, resulting in 2.6 million deaths per year. Almost every five seconds, a child dies from hunger-related diseases.

According to a 2009 World Bank report on Central Asia, almost 30 percent of people in Central Asia and Europe either live in poverty or are at risk of living in poverty. It is speculated that approximately 5 million people fall further below the poverty line for every 1 percent decline in gross domestic product (GDP). Meanwhile, according to an Asian Development Bank regional MDG Report of 2011, some 6 million people in Central Asia live in poverty, and recent United Nations predictions estimate that the number of people in Europe and Central Asia living on less than $1.25 per day increased by one million in 2009. It further says if high commodity prices persist, it is estimated that an additional 5.3 million people could slip into poverty (measured at $2.50 per day) because of higher food and fuel inflation, increasing the rate of extreme poverty from 5.5 to 6.7 percent over 2000 levels. According to the ILO's Word of the Work Report of 2011, in Central and South East Europe and the Commonwealth of Independent States, youth unemployment declined to 9.6 percent, after peaking in 2009 at 10.4 percent - the highest regional rate in the world.

Poverty in Canada has increased because of the recession in the post Afghanistan and Iraq war. During 2007-2009, the poverty rate in Canada had risen to 11.7 percent in 2009, an increase of over 900,000 Canadians compared to 2007. In her article, Poverty in Canada has increased as a result of the recession, published in Digital Journal on May 5, 2010, Stephanie Dearing writes, "The child poverty rate has likely risen to at least 12 percent, an increase of 160,000 children, compared to 2007. In October 2009, this meant 777,400 unemployed Canadians were not receiving benefits."

In the US, according to an RT web-site analysis, poverty is about to hit its highest level since 1965. It is predicted that by the end of 2014, poverty in the United States will be more prevalent than it was at the end of World War II. In 2010, the rate was 15.1 percent, meaning it would only need to increase by 0.1 per cent to surpass the worst that Americans have faced since 1965 - but this year, the poverty level is estimated to rise to 15.7 percent. The Poverty web site reports that the unemployment rate for 16- to 24-year-olds, which was 12 percent in 2004, had risen sharply from 15 percent in 2008 to 19 percent in 2009, and then reached 20 percent in 2010.

Social Watch (Novib, European union: unemployment and poverty, Social Watch, 1995) mentions that approximately 18 million people were unemployed in the European Union in 1994, comprising almost 11 percent of the total workforce on the continent. Meanwhile, the "unemployment rate for 16- to 24-year-olds in the UK has become highest in the West at 22 percent.

According to a research paper by Jinjun Xue and others, published in AEJ, (Xue Jinjun, et al, Unemployment, poverty and income disparity in urban China, AEJ, 2003) the urban unemployment rate in China reached 11.6 percent in 1999 and was a major cause of urban poverty. China is facing a higher rate of urban poverty every year. Although poverty has decreased in China from 85 percent in 1981 to 13.1 percent in 2008, the income disparities have increased. In China, 172 million people live below the line of poverty.

Adele Horin of the Sydney Morning Herald writes that two million Australians - or one in 10 - live below the poverty line. Approximately 54 percent of unemployed adults cannot afford at least three essentials of life. These life essentials in the Australian perspective include appropriate housing, secure home life and dental heath.However, around 74 percent of people below the poverty line are from jobless households.

Even after huge international and multilateral development intervention in Afghanistan at the opportunity cost of the developed world's own population, 36 percent of the Afghans are unemployed and live below poverty line. This is due to short-sighted and ad-hoc intervention planning in which the realities of Afghanistan in itself and the broader interests of Afghan people were not associated with the international interests. According to 2006 Annual Report of UNICEF, the under-5 mortality rate is 257 in every 1,000 live births. An overall life expectancy is 43. The country has adult literacy of 28 percent, out of which the youth literacy ratio for males is 51 percent and for females is 18 percent.

What Should Be Done?

There is a wide arena of inter- as well as intra-allies disagreements, contradictions, policy gaps, and governance as well as implementation fallouts. The solutions to the Afghan crises can only come out amid these gray areas and fallouts.

Pakistan has been the important cornerstone for the major fallouts in Afghanistan. While assessing Pakistan's destabilizing role in the region, particularly in Afghanistan, ISAF was correct in reaching the conclusions that Pakistan was behind almost every resistance in Afghanistan. General McChrystal's report in August 2009 linked all major Afghan insurgent groups to Pakistan and mentioned that senior leadership purportedly resided there and was connected to Al Qaeda. According to General McChrystal, elements within ISI supported these groups. Amid such a situation, Pakistan and the United States have undergone three years of antagonism (2009-2012), which caused blockage of the Torkham Gate border route, a route through which 25 percent of ISAF's non-lethal cargo was transported daily. By this, Pakistan wanted to assert its own strategic importance to the United States and other ISAF allies, and wanted to remind the world powers of their almost unavoidable dependency on Pakistan regarding Afghanistan. Nevertheless, the strategic plea of Pakistan was unrealistic and fallacious since Afghanistan could have also connected through Russia and Iran.

Most of the opinion polls and surveys have been faulty readings of the people in Pakistan concerning their opinions towards the United States. Most of them had the technical faults in the demography of the respondent selection. A Gallup Survey conducted in 2009 revealed that 59 percent of all Pakistanis believed the United States posed the greatest threat, while only 11 percent thought the Taliban to be a risk. However, the material reality is different in that the majority of ethnic Sindhi, Siraiki, Baloch and Pashtuns of plain areas and desert areas actually dislike Taliban and have no particular contempt toward the United States.

Three things collide together in Afghanistan: the transition of power in Afghanistan, elections in Afghanistan, and negotiations with the Taliban. The transition essentially requires a broader cooperation among all parties; however, the destabilizing parties like Pakistan may want to take advantage of the vacuum. Although the policy of gradual withdrawal of ISAF is important, the most important concern is that there are chances for Taliban and their associated terrorists to seize the opportunity for making gradual inroads in a post-ISAF situation. The role of capability in the Afghan National Army and security system would be tested.

According to Tim Sullivan's report "Indo-Pakistan proxy war in Afghanistan" in the Associated Press, the United States' backing of recent Kabul-Taliban talks and its openness to allowing some Taliban to join the Afghan government have led New Delhi to threaten forming a coalition with Iran, as well as Russia and Central Asian states who are averse to seeing the Taliban poised to takeover.

The basic drawback of the situation is that the international community has given lesser importance to local capacity for governance over the last 11 years engagement in Afghanistan. If the affairs of Afghanistan had been of gradual self-rule since 2001-2002, the international forces would not have opted for such a failure-like endgame. Had there been an indigenously initiated and supported mechanism of an electoral system, there would not have been local support for the insurgency. Besides, the ethnic composition of the statehood in the multi-ethnic societies and the balance of power between central, provincial and local/tribal governance have always played the role of key importance in the fragile states like Afghanistan. The investment and strengthening of local governance in Afghanistan is a matter of prime importance in the post-2014 scenario.

Once again, after ISAF withdrawal, Russia would be the loser, as most other parties would be following the United States. The situation will leave Russia alone to deal with the Taliban threat. In case of a Taliban return to power, drug trafficking and Islamist militancy in Central Asian states and Russia would destabilize ex-Soviet states and economies.

The ISAF withdrawal and Afghan elections will occur in the same year. This strategic juncture will require elections that are more transparent so that the process of transition could further be strengthened. Moreover, the major task for Afghan people and engaged international community is to carry on an appropriate state building process in which proportionate participation of all ethnicities is ensured. The inclusion of liberal Afghans in the new state is a condition that should not be compromised in any way.

There is another and highly important viewpoint in the world, mostly voiced by the broader left, right, and anti-war activists. It is based on the basic notion that no country has a right to invade any other country on any pretext. According to Echech a la Guerre, based on principals, this school of thought professes that "The war in Afghanistan is not a just war; the invasion of Afghanistan was never authorized by the Security Council and cannot be justified by invoking self-defence."

Historically, the people surrounding Afghanistan's borders have been pushed toward so-called Islamism since the 1970s. A minority of armed or state-supported religious extremists have dominated the liberal, secular, and progressive view of the majority. The worst impacts of *Talibanisation* have been especially present in the three liberal and secular majority provinces of Sindh, Baluchistan, Khyber Pakhtunkhuwa of Pakistan, the Xinhua province of China, Tajikistan, and Uzbekistan, along with India and Bangladesh as well. In fact, Sindh, the only secular province of Pakistan, has suffered a lot regarding the events in Afghanistan.

The British invaded the sovereign and independent Sindh in 1843 because Tzar's Russia was invading Central Asia in a bid to finally invade Afghanistan for their access to the hot waters of the Indian Ocean through Sindh. Sindh is not a country today despite its hundreds of years of countryhood, and it has suffered extraordinarily from the demographics, resources, and gradual inroads of the *Talibanisation* perspective. If Sindh becomes *Talibanised,* as desired by the Punjabi-dominated Pakistan establishment, the whole of *Southasia* would heavily feel the burns of the disaster of the radicalized *Islamization*. It is therefore imperative for the global community to take all necessary initiatives for quarantining, if not deleting, the epicentre of the terrorism virus in *Southasia*.

If such a noble task is achieved through the ISAF, through intervention and a strategically cohesive withdrawal, the possibility of new politics may begin in the region while minimizing chances of military dictatorships, as well as the dominance of security regimes on the civilian populations, especially in Pakistan. It could also broaden space for the still-surviving voice of a liberal, secular, and progressive majority.

It is important to focus on the intervention by the United Nations in such kinds of global interventions. The issue of Afghanistan has many aspects, but essentially, from the structural point of view, it is the issue of appropriate ethnic accommodation in the state field. A similar situation is also prevailing in Pakistan, where dominancy of ethnic Punjabi in association with an Urdu-speaking privileged community has perverted the society in name of *Islamization* so that Punjab may carry on its colonization of Sindh, Baluchistan, and to a certain extent, KP in Pakistan. In so many manners, if the chemistry of statecraft in Pakistan is not changed, the issue of Afghanistan will never get resolved.

The principle stance of antiwar activists is undoubtedly correct, however the Pandora's Box of the four-decade-long engagements with Afghanistan and Pakistan by the global community has torn apart the fabric of the sociopolitical ecology in the region enough that it needs a sustained settlement of the core issues. If the fate of Afghanistan is left solely to the regional counties, Afghanistan will never calm down. A global consensus over Afghanistan and surgical reforms in the Pakistani statehood is needed. The future of Afghanistan depends on the will of the Afghan majority as well as state-chemistry change in Pakistan.

Published in Truthout USA on October 23, 2013

16
NEIGHBOURLY ADVICE

Nepal is undergoing a socio-political transformation amid a highly contested debate around federalism and ethnicity to restructure statehood, governance and the future. The constitutional blind alley is a narrow strip between directionless sailing and rudderless anarchy. However, the forces of integration are stronger enough to ensure a safe voyage. Contrary to the established parameters for ethnic identity, popular discourse and semi-academic narrative around federalism portrays the terms "ethnicity" and "clan-identification" as being almost interchangeable. This is because, unlike India and Pakistan, Nepal has never undergone colonialism which helped cement ethnic and national entities in the federating provinces.

Myth of ethnicity

Nepal's ethnic discourse is not all about ethnicity as such. It is about a social entity blended of caste, clan and lingual peculiarities. If the Nepali definition of ethnicity is adopted, almost every province or state in India, Pakistan, Afghanistan and Iran will have more than 100 ethnic groups. The case of Nepal resembles that of Khyber Pakhtunkhuwa (KPK) and Balochistan in Pakistan, Sistan in Iran, Helmand in Afghanistan, and Kashmir and Himachal Pradesh in India. If the Nepali version of ethnicity is applied there, every district of these states will be having at least a dozen "ethnicities". Ethnic Pashtuns of KPK are socio-graphically similar to the Nepali people. They have many clans, languages and dialects. Besides, a majority of the highland languages are unintelligible to one another and the rest. They are a recognised ethnicity sociologically.

Nepal has, no doubt, its own ethnographical peculiarities; but use of the term "nationality" by some researchers for a clan-based distinct identity is a fallacy. Ethno-clan would be more suitable if "ethnicity" has become the popular term here. The term Nepali, however, is not an exclusively single ethnicity as it consists of some broader ethno-linguistic identities. Ethno-linguistically, the broader fold of cultural identities in Nepal has three demographic features — Indo-Nepali people of the Indo-European group of languages in the lowlands, valleys and Tarai plains; Tibeto-Nepalis of the Tibeto-Burman group of languages in the northern highlands; and indigenous Nepalis of various indigenous groups of languages in parts of the Tarai and other areas. Out of the 92 identified languages, 11 are spoken by 96.5 percent of the population including Nepali, Tharu, Bhojpuri, Tamang, Maithili, Magar, Awadhi, Nepal Bhasa, Rai, Limbu and Bajka. However, Nepali alone is spoken by 80 percent of the people. No doubt, these languages qualify for official status. Besides, the religious foundations of society are cohesive with 90.9 percent of the people following culturally similar Hinduism and Buddhism.

Development disparities

The discourse around ethnic federalism gives a feeling there are development disparities, poverty of opportunities and a contest to get an appropriate or more than an appropriate share. Clans like Khas and Newar have historically remained privileged by being part of statecraft; however, the trend has gradually changed after the comprehensive peace accord. Some research studies also mention that Madhesi and Tharu in the Tarai and Kham Magar in the mid-western hills along with some other clans have been underprivileged to a higher degree. Besides, there are many marginalised clans of Adivasis that have been officially recognised as being outside the Hindu caste system with some other indigenous communities like Raute, Chepang and Bankaria.

The context of state building sometimes becomes more important especially when a diverse socio-cultural web is seen in the perspective of federalisation. In such a situation, shaping conducive, efficient and diversity housing systems based on recognition of identities, national building, even development, urbanisation and industrialisation, and finally positive discrimination for the underdeveloped, unrepresented and marginalised become the only way forward.

There are many federal structures that need to be analysed. Societies with a complex web of ethnicities, cultures or demographics may have two to three demographic tiers of division along with four to six administrative tiers based on ethnicity, subculture, history, terrain, economic viability and administrative factors. This has been a common foundation of federal systems in *Southasia*, and some African countries including Ethiopia. Ethiopia has 80 smaller and bigger ethnic groups mostly based on the ethno-clan fabric. It is divided into 11 federating provinces which are mostly administrative. Each province has a few divisions, each of which is divided into districts. The district-level tiers are of ethnic basis, but the identity of the ethnicities is recognised constitutionally. Besides, the system is further divided in sub-districts and community-union levels.

Unlike Ethiopia, Pakistan consists of historically sovereign provinces. A couple of decades ago, Hindko, Potohari and Seraikis were living in their separate divisions within the respective provinces. Since the abolition of the divisional tier during General Pervez Musharraf's military rule, a discourse of new provinces has strengthened among these ethnicities. Indian federalism is relatively successful because of sustained democracy. Meanwhile, the political system in Bangladesh is based on divisions and districts. The divisions are mostly administrative and sub-cultural.

Towards possibilities

Society is the mother organisation. Sub-organisations like the state, political parties and institutions are always reflective of it, which is vice versa too. Nations should take the moment of state building and transformation as an opportunity and celebration as it comes after decades of struggle. The Nepali people should take it carefully and devise a federal system according to their own realities, interests and will.

In these political hot waters, some points of consensus are required. A proper solution to the current deadlock of legality and political precedence for choosing a Constituent Assembly or a regular Parliament, retaining the existing number or redefining the numerical limits of the seats and a new road map among the political parties for writing the constitution. This demands a role of academia, civil society and political think tanks. Historical nationhood and the virtue of invincibility are the foundations on which an appropriate federal system and uninterrupted democracy will lead Nepal as a growing and developing country.

Published in daily Kathmandu Post on September 7, 2012

17
RELIEF UNDER WATER

It was in 2010 that a great flood in *Southasia* inundated plains and valleys on both sides of the Indus River. We took initiatives to give maximum relief to the population hit by the disaster in the Sindh and Balochistan provinces in Pakistan, which was our intervention area as civil society actors. On our request, Kanak Mani Dixit together with the *Southasia*n Trust based in Nepal established the Indus Flood Relief Fund in Kathmandu. We were also supported by other *Southasia*ns as well as by the American Jewish World Service.

Unfortunately, all our efforts in Sindh and Balochistan encountered resistance by the establishment, which not only had problems with the initiatives taken by the Sindhi society for their people's humanitarian support during a disaster, but with our reaching out outside Pakistan without the nod of the Pakistani establishment. Now, floods have hit Pakistan again, worsening the lives of those who live in central and southern Punjab and in Sindh.

Dubious measures

In 2010, the civil and military establishment in the centre was trying their best to reduce the number of flood victims in Sindh in reports and data they shared with the international humanitarian community. Besides, they diverted floodwaters to save a maximum of military installations in Sindh at the cost of people and even inundated some areas deliberately for 'strategic reasons'. This resulted in an actual increase in the number of flood affected people and Internally Displaced People (IDP) by nearly ten million according to the Sindh Government and by around seven million according to the Islamabad based ethnically monotonous National Disaster Management Committee (NDMC).

The great flood of the Indus River in 2010 re-wrote the socio-economic and political history of the Sindhi people. The worst ever shock received by the people of Sindh was, when a Karachi based ethnic-political party, claiming to represent the Urdu speaking refugees who migrated to Sindh after 1947, practically resisted temporary migration of the flood affected Sindhi to Karachi despite the fact that a large part of the Indus plains in Sindh was under water.

There was yet another rainfall-induced flooding in 2011, but lower in scale than the previous, inundating only the Sindh province. NDMC, a government body authorised to communicate with the international donor agencies and the UN for disaster relief activities, neither took the initiative for relief operations nor did it ask the international funding community for humanitarian intervention in Sindh.

Inexcusable delay

In a workshop organised by Oxfam GB in Islamabad in 2011, civil-society representatives from various parts of Pakistan sat along with the international humanitarian community. As a participant in the workshop I seized the opportunity to ask Timo Pakkala, UN Country Representative in Pakistan, about the reasons behind their unexpected delay of nearly two months in taking an initiative for relief and rehabilitation activities, during which hundreds died and hundreds of thousands became homeless and had to live under the open sky. He replied that the UN actually could intervene without seeking the nod from Pakistan authorities; however due to various reasons they had waited for the Pakistani authorities' request. I confronted others with the same question, among whom was a representative of Church World Service (CWS), a Westerner. He told the participants that when he actively contacted the authorities in Islamabad and told them that CWS was willing to undertake relief activities in Sindh. But a bureaucrat told him that his keenness for relief activities indicated that he was a sympathiser of the Jeay Sindh (a term used in Pakistan for Sindhi secessionists). Thus, CWS also kept away.

Indian newspapers these days publish a lot of news about the Indian Army's and Air Force's rescue operations in the flood hit state of Jammu and Kashmir. The Indian Prime Minister Narendra Modi has also gracefully written to his Pakistani counterpart Nawaz Sharif that India would agree to undertake relief and rescue operations in Pakistan held Kashmir. In 2006, India had no doubt delivered great relief to the Pakistani side of Kashmir during the earthquake that affected almost the whole of Pakistan's North.

This again reminds me of the Indus Floods in 2010 and the Sindh Floods in 2011. In 2010, Pakistani armed forces, at one point, stopped the rescue operations and asked the Sindh Government to clear the bills for those operations that included the cost of boats, helicopters and vehicle utilisation as well as the services of the Army. In 2011, the armed forces did not even move to undertake rescue operations in Sindh. That's why, when I said emotionally at a forum, that if our Army could not help the people of Sindh we would be justified to request troops from the Indian authorities to rescue our people. This led to a visit of Pakistani military officials to our office by late 2011. It started with a hot tempered exchange of words, suddenly turning into threats directed at us. Due to our stance as civil, political and minority rights activists we were left with no other option than to close down The Institute for Social Movement, Pakistan and seek refuge out of the country.

Join forces

Gushing waters of five rivers of Punjab and the mighty Indus have again inundated Punjab and Sindh recently. Pakistani newspapers again have been telling the same old stories about IDPs as well as inundations of human settlements as a side-effect of efforts to save the military installations. The situation is bound to create another humanitarian crisis. This time, civil actors seeking to support flood affected people, the Pakistani authorities, the world humanitarian's community and the United Nations Office for the Coordination of Humanitarian Affairs (UN-OCHA) need to be both wise and bold to avoid repeating past blunders.

At the same time, the *Southasia*n countries need to establish a *Southasia*n Humanitarian Fund as well as a mechanism to jointly fight the aftermaths of natural disasters. In this regard, India, being the leading country of *Southasia*, together with Nepal, being a virtual capital of *Southasia*n initiatives, can do a lot by bringing all the other countries of the region together for such a noble cause. Would Saarc kindly stand up and show that it is not only a forum of *Southasia*n states, but one of and for the *Southasia*n people as well?

Published in daily The Kathmandu Post, Nepal on September 28, 2014